The New York Times

IN THE HEADLINES

Big Pharma

THE MONEY BEHIND THE PILLS

EDUCATIONAL PUBLISHING BOOKS

THE NEW YORK TIMES EDITORIAL STAFF

Published in 2020 by New York Times Educational Publishing
in association with The Rosen Publishing Group, Inc.
29 East 21st Street, New York, NY 10010

First Edition

The New York Times
Alex Ward: Editorial Director, Book Development
Phyllis Collazo: Photo Rights/Permissions Editor
Heidi Giovine: Administrative Manager

Rosen Publishing
Megan Kellerman: Managing Editor
Brandon Battersby: Editor
Greg Tucker: Creative Director
Brian Garvey: Art Director

Cataloging-in-Publication Data
Names: New York Times Company.
Title: Big pharma: the money behind the pills / edited by the New York Times editorial staff.
Description: New York : New York Times Educational Publishing, 2020. | Series: In the headlines | Includes glossary and index.
Identifiers: ISBN 9781642822069 (library bound) | ISBN 9781642822052 (pbk.) | ISBN 9781642822076 (ebook)
Subjects: LCSH: Pharmaceutical industry—United States—Juvenile literature. | Drugs—Research—Juvenile literature.
Classification: LCC RS67.U6 B54 2020 | DDC 615.1—dc23

Manufactured in the United States of America

On the cover: Behind-the-counter medications at a pharmacy in Brooklyn; Nicole Craine/The New York Times.

Contents

CHAPTER 2

Monopolies and Exclusivity Drive Price Spikes

CHAPTER 3

Disease Branding and the Profusion of Diagnoses

CHAPTER 4

The Money Behind Epidemics: Preventing, Treating and Healing

Introduction

AS AMERICANS, WE SPEND the most on prescription drugs of any nation in the world — double the national average spent in other developed countries. The pharmaceutical industry makes significant profits from the American market: The top ten public U.S. pharmaceutical manufacturers made $67.8 billion after taxes in 2016.

Despite this lucrative industry and high costs to consumers, Big Pharma has continued to seek ever-higher profits. In one extreme case in 2015, the price of one drug rose from $13.50 a tablet to $750 overnight, drawing national attention. Big Pharma has also been criticized for its role in the United States' opioid epidemic, which involves a cycle of doctors prescribing addictive painkillers to patients long-term, generating money for pharmaceutical companies while patients and their loved ones suffer. Situations such as these, along with high insurance premiums, are stark realities many Americans face to get the medications they need. They have created an ominous, often hostile relationship between the pharmaceutical industry and doctors and their patients.

The term "Big Pharma" itself has come to evoke thoughts of greedy companies that put profits ahead of people's health. But, like any industry, drug manufacturers are in the business of selling products and turning a profit. Many companies do play fair, while others exploit publicly funded programs and loopholes in the very laws that have been written to protect consumers and stimulate drug innovation.

How does one industry accomplish this?

Big Pharma found its legs in the early 1980s after the Bayh-Dole Act was passed. The law was intended to mitigate the risk of developing new drugs and technology for companies by granting them exclusive

GEORGE ETHEREDGE FOR THE NEW YORK TIMES

The headquarters of Purdue Pharma in Stamford, Conn. Federal prosecutors said the company knew of "significant" abuse of OxyContin soon after it came on the market, but hid that information. States and cities have filed a wave of lawsuits against Purdue Pharma and other opioid manufacturers and distributors.

rights to sell their products, and by extending their patents to see more return on the money spent on research and development (R&D). The law contributed to stunting new drug development because companies were incentivized to cash in on one blockbuster drug and hold onto its "exclusivity" for decades before a generic version or something better entered the market.

Additionally, publicly funded research dollars through the National Institutes of Health (N.I.H.) and its divisions, such as the National Cancer Institute (N.C.I.), encouraged many pharmaceutical companies to sit on the sidelines and let academia and taxpayers front the cost, essentially having the public do the heavy lifting of R&D.

Thus, with little risk, drug manufacturers have been capitalizing on acquiring new drugs and smaller manufacturers. They have been able to increase the prices of exclusive drugs because there is a captive market; the sick absolutely need them, and insurers and programs like Medicare are prevented from negotiating lower drug prices. Many Americans only see the low copay costs of prescriptions, while the system is sustained on taxpayer dollars and on insurance companies that need to raise premiums to cover their liability.

With the price of pills reaching an all-time high, people are turning to the U.S. government for solutions. As a result, the squeeze from Big Pharma became a top concern in the 2016 election and remains a stress point for the Trump administration today. The articles in this collection provide valuable coverage and insights into the practices of drug manufacturers, the driving forces behind the costs consumers face and what can be done to more effectively regulate Big Pharma.

CHAPTER 1

Big Pharma's New Deal: Acquisition and Little Innovation

Within the last two decades, one of the ways Big Pharma has made money is to not develop new drugs at all. Instead, big companies such as Pfizer and Valeant perfected a new model of acquiring smaller companies and funding academic research to mitigate the risks of bringing innovative medicines to the market. This chapter covers some of the biggest purchases of smaller companies by larger companies and demonstrates how publicly funded research generates more money for Big Pharma, but almost no innovation.

Blockbuster Drugs Are So Last Century

BY ALEX BERENSON | JULY 3, 2005

INDIANAPOLIS — Drug companies do an awful job of finding new medicines. They rely too much on billion-dollar blockbuster drugs that are both overmarketed and overprescribed. And they have been too slow to disclose side effects of popular medicines.

Typical complaints from drug industry critics, right? Well, yes. Only this time they come from executives at Eli Lilly, the sixth-largest American drug maker and the company that invented Prozac.

From this placid Midwestern city, well removed from the Boston-to-Washington corridor that is the core of the pharmaceutical industry, Lilly is ambitiously rethinking the way drugs are discovered and sold. In a speech to shareholders in April, Sidney Taurel, Lilly's chief executive, presented the company's new strategy in a pithy phrase: "the right dose of the right drug to the right patient at the right time."

In other words, Lilly sees its future not in blockbuster medicines like Prozac that are meant for tens of millions of patients, but rather in drugs that are aimed at smaller groups and can be developed more quickly and cheaply, possibly with fewer side effects.

There is no guarantee, of course, that Lilly will succeed. And some Wall Street analysts complain about the recent track record of the company, saying that it has habitually overpromised the potential of its drugs and taken one-time charges that distort its reported profits. In the last year, Lilly's stock has fallen 21 percent, while shares in the average big drug maker have been flat.

Still, since late 2001, Lilly's labs have produced five truly new drugs, including treatments for osteoporosis, depression and lung cancer. The total exceeds that of many of its much-larger competitors. And at a time when the drug industry seems adrift, that Lilly has any vision at all for the future is striking.

"The challenge for us as an industry, as a company, is to move more from a blockbuster model to a targeted model," Mr. Taurel said at Lilly's headquarters here recently. "We need a better value proposition than today."

For five years, drug companies have struggled to bring new medicines to market. But Lilly executives say they believe that the drought is not permanent. Advances in understanding the ways that cells and genes work will soon lead to important new drugs, said Peter Johnson, executive director of corporate strategy.

Moreover, Lilly expects that drug makers without breakthrough medicines that are either the first or the best in their categories will face increasing pressure from insurers to cut prices or lose coverage.

If that vision is correct, the industry's winners will be companies that invest heavily in research and differentiate themselves by focusing on a few diseases instead of on building size and cutting costs through mergers, as Pfizer has done. Lilly, which spends nearly 20 percent of its sales on research, compared with about 16 percent for the average drug company, may be well positioned for the future.

"We do not believe that size pays off for anybody, especially size acquired in an acquisition," Mr. Taurel said.

But if Lilly is wrong about the industry's direction, or if its research efforts fail, it could wind up like Merck, the third-biggest American drug company, which has also adamantly opposed mergers and bet instead on its labs. After its own eight-year drought of major new drugs, Merck has had a 65 percent decline in its stock price since 2000, and its chief executive was forced out in May.

Mr. Johnson acknowledges that Lilly's strategy is risky. "You can't make a discovery operation invent what you want them to invent," he said.

So Lilly is seeking to improve its odds and to cut research costs by changing the way it develops drugs, said Dr. Steven M. Paul, president of the company's laboratories.

Bringing a drug to market cost more than $900 million on average in 2003, compared with $230 million in 1987, according to estimates from Lilly and industry groups. But the public's willingness to accept side effects is shrinking, and some drug-safety experts and lawmakers want even larger and longer clinical trials for new drugs, increasing development costs. If nothing changes, Lilly expects that by 2010, the cost of finding a single new drug may reach $2 billion, an unsustainable amount, Dr. Paul said.

"We've got to do something to reduce the costs," he added.

The biggest expense in drug development comes not from early-stage research, he said, but from the failure of drugs after they have left the labs and been tested in humans. A drug that has moved into first-stage human clinical trials now has only about an 8 percent chance of reaching the market. Even in late-stage trials, about half of all drugs fail, often because they do not prove better than existing treatments.

To change that, Lilly is focusing its research efforts on finding biomarkers — genes or other cellular signals that will indicate which patients are most likely to respond to a given drug. Other drug makers are also searching for biomarkers, but Lilly executives are the most vocal in expressing their belief that this area of research will fundamentally change the way drugs are developed.

Using biomarkers should make drugs more effective and reduce side effects, Dr. Paul said. If all goes as planned, the company will know sooner whether its drugs are working, and will develop fewer drugs that fail in clinical trials. The company may even be able to use shorter, smaller clinical trials because its drugs will demonstrate their effectiveness more quickly.

To improve its chances further, Lilly has focused its research efforts on four types of diseases: diabetes, cancer, mental illness and some heart ailments. In each category, it has had a history of successful drugs.

The company hopes to reduce the cost of new development to about $700 million a drug by 2010. Because Lilly now spends about $2.7 billion annually on research, that figure would imply that the company could develop as many as four new drugs a year, compared with just one a year if current trends do not change.

Among the company's most promising drugs in development are ruboxistaurin, for diabetes complications; arzoxifene, for the prevention of osteoporosis and breast cancer; and enzastaurin, for brain tumors and other cancers.

The flip side of Lilly's plan is that drugs it develops may be used more narrowly than current treatments. For example, the company may find that a diabetes drug works best in patients under 40 with a specific genetic marker, and enroll only those patients in its clinical trials. While doctors can legally prescribe any medicine for any reason once it is on the market, insurers would probably balk at covering the drug for diabetics over 40 or for patients without the genetic marker.

"The old model was, one size fits a whole lot of people," said Mr. Johnson, Lilly's strategist.

Last month, Lilly's vision of targeted therapies gained some ground — albeit at another company. The Food and Drug Administration approved BiDil, a heart drug from NitroMed that is intended for use by African-Americans. The approval, based on a clinical trial that enrolled only black patients, was the first ever for a drug meant for one racial group. While race can be a crude characterization of groups, it can serve as an effective biomarker, scientists said.

Lilly's road map may look appealing. But some analysts question whether the company is as different from the rest of the industry as it would like to believe.

While it professes to see a future of narrowly marketed medicines, Lilly is more dependent than any other major drug maker on a single blockbuster drug: Zyprexa, its treatment for schizophrenia and manic depression. Zyprexa accounted for about $4.4 billion in sales last year, 30 percent of the company's total sales.

And while Lilly executives say they want to avoid marketing its drugs too heavily or in anything less than a forthright way, federal prosecutors in Philadelphia are investigating its marketing practices for Zyprexa and Prozac. Last month, Lilly said it would pay $690 million to settle 8,000 lawsuits that contended that Zyprexa could cause obesity and diabetes and that the company had not properly disclosed that risk.

Lilly says that it acted properly in marketing Zyprexa and that is cooperating with the federal investigation. Still, the controversy has hurt Zyprexa sales, which fell 8 percent in the United States last year.

Some of Lilly's newest drugs have been commercial disappointments. The company and analysts hoped that annual sales of Xigris, a treatment introduced in late 2001 for a blood infection called sepsis, could reach $1 billion; Xigris's sales were $200 million last year. Sales of Strattera, for attention deficit disorder, slowed after a report in December that the drug can cause a rare but serious form of liver damage.

Michael Krensavage, an analyst at Raymond James & Associates who rates Lilly shares as underperform, said that Lilly's emphasis on targeted therapies might be a defensive response to the industry's recent inability to produce blockbusters.

Rather than targeted treatments, "drug companies would hope to produce a medicine that works for everybody," Mr. Krensavage said. "That's certainly the goal."

Mr. Krensavage also criticized Lilly's accounting, noting that the company has taken one-time charges in each of the last three years that have muddied its financial results. Lilly said its accounting complied with all federal rules.

Despite the company's recent stumbles with Zyprexa, other analysts say Lilly is well positioned, and they praise Mr. Taurel for looking for innovative ways to lower the cost of drug development.

"Sidney has a better concept of what's happening outside his four walls and is far better in reflecting that in how the company runs on a day-to-day basis than any of his peers," said Richard Evans, an analyst at Sanford C. Bernstein & Company.

Mr. Taurel acknowledged Lilly's dependence on Zyprexa and the fact that some new drugs had not met expectations. But he said the transition to targeted therapies would take years, if not decades. With earnings last year of $3.1 billion, before one-time charges, and no major patent expirations before 2011, Lilly can afford to make long-term bets, he said. "Our model needs to evolve," he said. "For the industry and for Lilly."

When Academia Puts Profit Ahead of Wonder

BY JANET RAE-DUPREE | SEPT. 6, 2008

> *It is the policy and objective of the Congress to use the patent system to promote the utilization of inventions arising from federally supported research or development" and "to promote collaboration between commercial concerns and nonprofit organizations, including universities.*
>
> *— The Bayh-Dole Act, a k a the University Small Business Patent Procedures Act*

THE LAW OF unintended consequences is perhaps less a "law" than a simple statement of fact: We cannot accurately predict all the results of our actions. We may do something with the best of intentions, and sometimes even accomplish the good toward which we aim. Yet, at the same time, we are all too often surprised by results that didn't occur to us beforehand.

The Bayh-Dole Act of 1980 started out with the best of intentions. By clearing away the thicket of conflicting rules and regulations at various federal agencies, it set out to encourage universities to patent and license results of federally financed research. For the first time, academicians were able to profit personally from the market transfer of their work. For the first time, academia could be powered as much by a profit motive as by the psychic reward of new discovery.

University "tech transfer" offices have boomed from a couple dozen before the law's passage to nearly 300 today. University patents have leapt a hundredfold. Professors are stepping away from the lab and lecture hall to navigate the thicket of venture capital, business regulations and commercial competition.

None of these are necessarily negative outcomes. But more than a quarter-century after President Jimmy Carter signed it into law, the Bayh-Dole Act, sponsored by the former Senators Birch Bayh,

Democrat of Indiana, and Robert Dole, Republican of Kansas, is under increasing scrutiny by swelling ranks of critics. The primary concern is that its original intent — to infuse the American marketplace with the fruits of academic innovation — has also distorted the fundamental mission of universities.

In the past, discovery for its own sake provided academic motivation, but today's universities function more like corporate research laboratories. Rather than freely sharing techniques and results, researchers increasingly keep new findings under wraps to maintain a competitive edge. What used to be peer-reviewed is now proprietary. "Share and share alike" has devolved into "every laboratory for itself."

In trying to power the innovation economy, we have turned America's universities into cutthroat business competitors, zealously guarding the very innovations we so desperately want behind a hopelessly tangled web of patents and royalty licenses.

Of course, there is precedent for scientific secrecy, notes Daniel S. Greenberg, author of "Science for Sale: The Perils, Rewards and Delusions of Campus Capitalism" (University of Chicago Press, 2007). When James Watson and Francis Crick were homing in on DNA's double-helix structure in the 1950s, they zealously guarded their work from prying eyes until they could publish their findings, to be certain that they would get the credit for making the discovery.

"They didn't try to patent it," Mr. Greenberg notes, "but somebody doing the same work today would certainly take a crack at patenting the double helix."

In fact, it was the life sciences — in particular, biotechnology — that started universities down the slippery commercial slope in the first place. Even before the Bayh-Dole Act, pharmaceutical companies were eagerly trolling campuses, looking for projects to finance. After the law was passed, they stepped up their efforts, but now with renewed zeal for keeping potential trade secrets from competitors.

While patients have benefited from the growing supply of new medications, the universities have obtained patents not only for the actual substances but also for the processes and methods used to make them, potentially hampering discovery of even more beneficial treatments.

"Bayh-Dole tore down the taboos that existed against universities engaging in overtly commercial activity. Universities really thought that they were going to make it rich," said Jennifer Washburn, author of "University Inc.: The Corporate Corruption of Higher Education" (Basic Books, 2005). "Each school was convinced that if they came up with that one blockbuster invention, they could solve all their financial problems."

Ms. Washburn says that was "extremely wrong-headed." Initially reacting to the law by slapping patents on every possible innovation, universities quickly discovered that patents were an expensive proposition. The fees and legal costs involved in obtaining a single patent can run upward of $15,000, and that doesn't count the salaries of administrative staff members. Instead of bringing home the bacon, university tech transfer offices were throwing money into the void with little hope of returns.

To date, Ms. Washburn says, data gathered by the Association of University Technology Managers, a trade group, show that fewer than half of the 300 research universities actively seeking patents have managed to break even from technology transfer efforts. Instead, two-thirds of the revenue tracked by the association has gone to only 13 institutions.

Part of the problem has been a lingering misunderstanding about where the value lies in innovation. Patenting a new basic science technique, or platform technology, puts it out of the reach of graduate students who might have made tremendous progress using it.

Similarly, exclusive licensing of a discovery to a single company thwarts that innovation's use in any number of other fields. R. Stanley Williams, a nanotechnologist from Hewlett-Packard, testified to Congress in 2002 that much of the academic research to which H.P. has had difficulty gaining access could be licensed to several companies without eroding its intellectual property value.

"Severe disagreements have arisen over conflicting interpretations of the Bayh-Dole Act," he said. "Large U.S.-based corporations have become so disheartened and disgusted with the situation, they are now working with foreign universities, especially the elite institutions in France, Russia and China."

The issue is further clouded by "reach through" licenses, complex arrangements used by many tech transfer offices. A reach-through lets the patent holder claim a share of any profits that result from using, say, an enabling technology, even if those profits come several steps down the market transfer line. Several universities are already embroiled in messy lawsuits trying to sort out who is entitled to what.

Perhaps the most troublesome aspect of campus commercialization is that research decisions are now being based on possible profits, not on the inherent value of knowledge. "Blue sky" research — the kind of basic experimentation that leads to a greater understanding of how the world works — has largely been set aside in favor of projects considered to have more immediate market potential.

In academia's continuing pursuit of profit, the wonder of simple serendipitous discovery has been left on the curb.

JANET RAE-DUPREE writes about science and emerging technology in Silicon Valley.

Grant System Leads Cancer Researchers to Play It Safe

BY GINA KOLATA | JUNE 27, 2009

AMONG THE RECENT research grants awarded by the National Cancer Institute is one for a study asking whether people who are especially responsive to good-tasting food have the most difficulty staying on a diet. Another study will assess a Web-based program that encourages families to choose more healthful foods.

Many other grants involve biological research unlikely to break new ground. For example, one project asks whether a laboratory discovery involving colon cancer also applies to breast cancer. But even if it does apply, there is no treatment yet that exploits it.

The cancer institute has spent $105 billion since President Richard M. Nixon declared war on the disease in 1971. The American Cancer Society, the largest private financer of cancer research, has spent about $3.4 billion on research grants since 1946.

Yet the fight against cancer is going slower than most had hoped, with only small changes in the death rate in the almost 40 years since it began.

One major impediment, scientists agree, is the grant system itself. It has become a sort of jobs program, a way to keep research laboratories going year after year with the understanding that the focus will be on small projects unlikely to take significant steps toward curing cancer.

"These grants are not silly, but they are only likely to produce incremental progress," said Dr. Robert C. Young, chancellor at Fox Chase Cancer Center in Philadelphia and chairman of the Board of Scientific Advisors, an independent group that makes recommendations to the cancer institute.

The institute's reviewers choose such projects because, with too little money to finance most proposals, they are timid about taking chances on ones that might not succeed. The problem, Dr. Young and

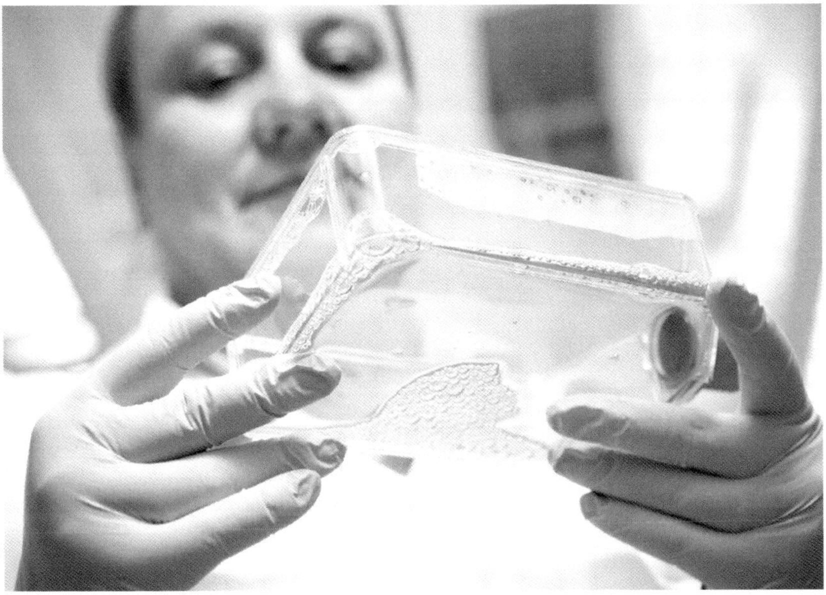

BRYCE VICKMARK FOR THE NEW YORK TIMES

Dr. Ewa T. Sicinska turned to a private foundation to finance her research.

others say, is that projects that could make a major difference in cancer prevention and treatment are all too often crowded out because they are too uncertain. In fact, it has become lore among cancer researchers that some game-changing discoveries involved projects deemed too unlikely to succeed and were therefore denied federal grants, forcing researchers to struggle mightily to continue.

Take one transformative drug, for breast cancer. It was based on a discovery by Dr. Dennis Slamon of the University of California, Los Angeles, that very aggressive breast cancers often have multiple copies of a particular protein, HER-2. That led to the development of herceptin, which blocks HER-2.

Now women with excess HER-2 proteins, who once had the worst breast cancer prognoses, have prognoses that are among the best. But when Dr. Slamon wanted to start this research, his grant was turned down. He succeeded only after the grateful wife of a patient helped him get money from Revlon, the cosmetics company.

Yet studies like the one on tasty food are financed. That study, which received a grant of $100,000 over two years, is based on the idea that since obesity is associated with an increased risk of cancer, understanding why people have trouble losing weight could lead to better weight control methods, which could lead to less obesity, which could lead to less cancer.

"It was the first grant I ever submitted, and it was funded on the first try," said the principal investigator, Bradley M. Appelhans, an assistant professor of basic medical sciences and psychology at the University of Arizona. Dr. Appelhans said he realized it would hardly cure cancer, but hoped that "it will provide knowledge that will incrementally contribute to more effective cancer prevention strategies."

Even top federal cancer officials say the system needs to be changed.

"We have a system that works over all pretty well, and is very good at ruling out bad things — we don't fund bad research," said Dr. Raynard S. Kington, acting director of the National Institutes of Health, which includes the cancer institute. "But given that, we also recognize that the system probably provides disincentives to funding really transformative research."

The private American Cancer Society follows a similarly cautious path. Last year, it awarded $124 million in new research grants, with some money coming from large donors but most from events like walkathons and memorial donations.

Dr. Otis W. Brawley, chief medical officer at the cancer society, said the whole cancer research effort remained too cautious.

"The problem in science is that the way you get ahead is by staying within narrow parameters and doing what other people are doing," Dr. Brawley said. "No one wants to fund wild new ideas."

He added that the problem of getting money for imaginative but chancy proposals had worsened in recent years. There are more scientists seeking grants — they surged into the field in the 1990s when the National Institutes of Health budget doubled before plunging again.

That makes many researchers, who need grants not just to run their labs but also sometimes to keep their faculty positions, even more cautious in the grant proposals they submit. And grant review committees become more wary about giving scarce money to speculative proposals.

Philanthropies, which helped some researchers try outside-the-box ideas, are now having financial problems. And advances in technology have made research more expensive.

"Scientists don't like talking about it publicly," because they worry that their remarks will be viewed as lashing out at the health institutes, which supports them, said Dr. Richard D. Klausner, a former director of the National Cancer Institute.

But, Dr. Klausner added: "There is no conversation that I have ever had about the grant system that doesn't have an incredible sense of consensus that it is not working. That is a terrible wasted opportunity for the scientists, patients, the nation and the world."

A BIG IDEA WITHOUT A BACKER

For 25 years, Eileen K. Jaffe received federal grants to run her lab. As a senior scientist at the Fox Chase Cancer Center, with a long list of published papers in prestigious journals, she is a respected, established researcher.

Then Dr. Jaffe stumbled upon results that went against textbook explanations, suggesting that it might be possible to find an entirely new class of drugs that could disable proteins that fuel cancer cells. Now she wants to find chemicals that might be developed into such drugs.

But her grant proposal was rejected out of hand by the institutes of health, not even discussed by a review panel. She had no preliminary data showing that the idea was likely to work, something reviewers always want to see, and the idea was just too unprecedented.

Dr. Jaffe epitomizes the scientist who realizes that if she were to single-mindedly pursue her unorthodox idea, her "career may be ruined in the process," in the words of Dr. Brawley of the American Cancer Society.

Dr. Jaffe is just conceiving her project; it is much to soon to know whether it will result in a revolutionary drug. And even if she does find potential new drugs, it is not clear that they will be effective. Most new ideas are difficult to prove, and most potential new drugs fail.

So Dr. Jaffe was not entirely surprised when her grant application to look for such cancer drugs was summarily rejected.

"They said I don't have preliminary results," she said. "Of course I don't. I need the grant money to get them."

Dr. Young, chancellor at Fox Chase, said Dr. Jaffe's situation showed why people with bold new ideas often just give up.

"You can't prove it will work in advance," he said. "If you could, it wouldn't be a high-risk idea."

It is a long haul, Dr. Jaffe knows. And she has already had to downsize her lab. But, she said, she will persist.

ANGELS OUTSIDE GOVERNMENT

At the Dana-Farber Cancer Institute in Boston, Dr. Ewa T. Sicinska knew she would have a similar problem with her research. She wanted to grow human cancers in mice. Unlike Dr. Jaffe, though, Dr. Sicinska did not even apply for government money.

It is not that the project was unimportant.

"Rather than have to start a human clinical trial to test new drugs, we want to test them first in mice with real human tumors," said Dr. George D. Demetri, who leads the research group supporting Dr. Sicinska.

Researchers have studied mouse cancers but, they acknowledge, they are just not the same as human cancers — they are much easier to treat, and drugs that cure mice often do nothing in people. So, over the years, scientists have tried to implant human cancer cells in mice, but with little success.

"Everyone told us that if you take tumors out of patients and put them in mice, they don't grow," Dr. Demetri said. The tumor cells usually were put in a plastic dish before being implanted in mice. "We said — wait a minute. The cells are not growing in the plastic dish. They probably are dying. What if we bypass the dish?' "

With that idea in mind, Dr. Demetri, convinced it was too speculative to get federal money, tapped an unusual source, the Ludwig Fund. Endowed by Daniel K. Ludwig, one of the world's richest men in the 1960s and 1970s, the fund supports unfettered cancer research at six medical centers in the United States, including Dana-Farber, to be used at the institutes' discretion. That put Dr. Sicinska in a very different position from that of Dr. Jaffe. She could try something chancy without a grant.

Dr. Sicinska used a quarter of a million dollars of Ludwig money for this project, buying mice without immune systems, which meant they could not reject human tumors, and housing them in a germ-free basement lab. She spent months learning to implant tumors in the mice and enlisted geneticists to study the implanted tumors, making sure they did not mutate beyond recognition.

She spends her days in the lab, using a miniature ultrasound machine to scan the mice, hairless creatures with prominent ears. Four types of sarcomas — cancers of fat, muscle or bone — are growing in them and look genetically identical to the tumors removed from patients.

Dr. Elias A. Zerhouni, former director of the National Institutes of Health, said he was not sure that a grant for the project would have been turned down. The N.I.H., he said, does finance research on mouse models for human cancer.

But Dr. Demetri said he did not apply "because we have lots of experience in what's fundable." His mouse work, he said, is exploratory, and he cannot predict what he will find or when. He certainly could not lay out a road map of what he would do and promise results in a few years.

STUDIES WITH A DIFFERENT GOAL

Researchers like Dr. Appelhans, who is studying weight control and tasty foods, do not expect to change the outlook for cancer patients anytime soon. But, they say, that does not mean their work is unimportant.

Dr. Appelhans will study 85 overweight or obese women, measuring how much the tastes and textures of food drive their eating. Then they will be given a weight loss diet and nutritional counseling. Dr. Appelhans will ask whether those who are most tempted by the tastes and textures also have the most trouble following the diet.

As for the grant to assess a Web-based program to improve food choices, it is predicated on studies indicating that what people eat in childhood and adolescence may have an impact on cancer risk in middle and old age, said the grant recipient, Karen Weber Cullen, associate professor of pediatrics at Baylor College of Medicine. Some studies have found that people who reported having eaten fruits and vegetables when they were younger and maintaining a healthy weight were less likely to have cancer.

Of course, it would not be feasible to follow participants for 30 or 40 years to see if their cancer risk was altered, Dr. Cullen noted. But, she added, "we try to achieve improvements in diet and physical activity

DAVID WALTER BANKS FOR THE NEW YORK TIMES

Dr. Otis W. Brawley, chief medical officer at the American Cancer Society, said the cancer research effort remained too cautious.

behaviors that become permanent and will make a difference in later years."

In the study asking whether a molecular pathway that spurs the growth of colon cancer cells also encourages the growth of breast cancer cells, the principal investigator ultimately wants to find a safe drug to prevent breast cancer. She received a typical-size grant of a little more than $1 million for the five-year study.

The plan, said the investigator, Louise R. Howe, an associate research professor at Weill Cornell Medical College, is first to confirm her hypothesis about the pathway in breast cancer cells. But even if it is correct, the much harder research would lie ahead because no drugs exist to block the pathway, and even if they did, there are no assurances that they would be safe.

Dr. Howe said she hoped that she would find such drugs, or that companies would. Then she wants to develop a way to selectively deliver the drugs to precancerous breast cells. If it all works and the treatment is safe, women with precancerous conditions could avoid developing cancer.

Dr. Howe has reviewed grants for the cancer institute herself, she said, and realizes that, among other things, those that get financed must have "a novel hypothesis that is credible based on what we know already."

TRYING TO CHANGE THE SYSTEM

The National Institutes of Health has started "pilot experiments" to see if there is a better way of getting financing for innovative projects, its acting director, Dr. Kington, said.

They include "pioneer awards," begun in 2004 for "ideas that have the potential for high impact but may be too novel, span too diverse a range of disciplines or be at a stage too early to fare well in the traditional peer review process." But only 3 percent to 5 percent of the applicants get funded. Now the institutes have decided to set aside up to $25 million for "transformative R01 grants," described as "proposing exceptionally innovative, high risk, original and/or unconventional research with the potential to create or overturn fundamental paradigms."

About 700 proposals have come in, but only a small number are expected to be financed, according to Dr. Keith R. Yamamoto, a molecular biologist and executive vice dean of the school of medicine at the University of California, San Francisco, and co-chairman of the committee that reviewed the proposals last week.

"From reading the applications so far, there are really some fantastic things," Dr. Yamamoto said.

There also is new money from the federal economic stimulus package passed by Congress, which gives the National Institutes of Health $200 million for "challenge grants" lasting two years or less.

But the N.I.H. has received about 21,000 applications for 200 challenge grants, and researchers who have applied concede there is not much hope.

"I did submit one of these challenge grants recently, like the rest of the lemmings," said Dr. Chi Dang, professor of medicine, cell biology, oncology and pathology at the Johns Hopkins University School of Medicine. But, he added, "there are many, many more applications than slots."

Some experienced scientists have found a way to offset the problem somewhat. They do chancy experiments by siphoning money from their grants.

"In a way, the system is encrypted," Dr. Yamamoto said, allowing those in the know to wink and do their own thing on the side.

Great discoveries have been made with N.I.H. financing without manipulating the system, Dr. Klausner said.

"But," he added, "I actually believe that by and large it is despite, rather than because of, the review system."

Are Doctors Too Wary of Drug Companies?

BY PAULINE W. CHEN, M.D. | OCT. 18, 2012

NOT LONG AGO, I asked a colleague for advice on a patient. He offered up a couple of treatment options, then stopped to show me a new medical app on his electronic tablet. With a few swipes of his finger, he summoned a compilation of research articles, synopses and even entire textbooks that, printed and bound, would have filled shelves in a library.

"But do you know what the best part is?" he asked with a twinkle in his eye. I thought of the exhaustive reference material and the seemingly endless scroll of diagnoses that were all so easy to access on the small screen balanced on his knees.

"The best part is that none of this is sponsored by Pharma!" he said with a broad smile. "There's no bias."

My colleague is not the only doctor who feels that way, according to a recent study published in The New England Journal of Medicine.

For years, most doctors have had a predictable, if not close, relationship with the pharmaceutical industry. Companies handed out office tchotchkes, paid for staff lunches and distributed drug samples for patients. More significantly, drug companies were important sources of biomedical research money, particularly during periods when federal support wavered. It was understood that the companies providing funding would leave the researchers alone to design and conduct the study, analyze the data and write up the results.

That understanding began to fray about a decade ago when doctors, and patients, began to realize that drug companies were becoming too involved with the research they were supporting. For example, one major pharmaceutical firm manipulated data and underestimated the risk of heart attacks, strokes and deaths in a large study of a drug for arthritis. The drug was eventually withdrawn from the market, but not before 80 million patients had used it, with annual sales topping $2.5 billion.

The case highlighted the dangers of industry sponsorship of research into new drugs, and the public became eager to expose any potential conflict of interest, particularly for doctors. Within a few years, a new standard of transparency in medicine emerged. Brightly labeled drug company pens became an embarrassment; lunches on the drug company tab and sponsored conferences turned suspect; and editors at numerous medical journals published lengthy screeds detailing their disclosure requirements.

The new skepticism and transparency were no doubt good for patients and doctors, but this recent study reveals that in our zeal to single out the pharmaceutical industry's biases, we may have become blind to our own.

The researchers created several hypothetical drug studies, then asked a group of practicing physicians to rate the "studies" and the likelihood they would prescribe the new "drug." The researchers purposefully varied the quality of the studies and the disclosures — some of the made-up studies disclosed that they had received pharmaceutical company funding, others said they'd received support from the National Institutes of Health, and the rest listed no funding disclosures at all.

Most of the doctors were able to assess the quality of the research pretty accurately. After reading the less rigorous studies, the ones that weren't designed, conducted or analyzed well, the doctors were hesitant to prescribe the new drugs under study; seeing the more rigorous studies, they were more willing to do so.

But the researchers also found that the doctors were also unduly swayed by any mention of industry funding. Regardless of the quality, if a study was supported by a pharmaceutical company, doctors were less willing to consider prescribing the studied drug and less likely to assess the quality of the research with accuracy.

"Some amount of skepticism is warranted," said Dr. Aaron S. Kesselheim, lead author of the study and an assistant professor of medicine in the division of pharmacoepidemiology and pharmacoeconomics at the Brigham and Women's Hospital in Boston. "But ultimately it should be the quality of the study and the impact of the results that determine your confidence about using a new drug, not who was funding it."

Being overly skeptical has serious implications for patient care. The pharmaceutical industry, along with medical device and biotechnology firms, continues to finance a majority of current research. In 2007, for example, industry was responsible for nearly 60 percent of the more than $100 billion spent on research. Much industry-supported research focuses on the side effects of new drugs. By writing off such research, doctors risk overlooking findings that may have important treatment implications for their patients, like a new cholesterol-lowering drug that is found to have less of an effect on energy and blood sugar levels than other similar medications.

Dr. Kesselheim and his collaborators believe what is needed in biomedical research is even greater transparency. Such openness would include more independent third-party statistical reviews to ensure that data is not being manipulated or misleading and wider use of public Web sites like ClinicalTrials.gov, regardless of the source of funding.

ClinicalTrials.gov lists study details like objectives, design and data gathered, providing doctors and patients alike with a way to confirm that no data is being selectively reported or distorted. But participation on the site is voluntary, and pharmaceutical, medical device and biomedical companies are often hesitant to share what they consider proprictary data, choosing instead to list only selective details, or no information at all.

Until full transparency is achieved and such details are available to all on the Web or for independent statistical reviews, Dr. Kesselheim and his collaborators suggest that both doctors and patients remain alert to potential biases — Big Pharma's, and also their own.

"Excessive skepticism," Dr. Kesselheim observed, "is as much a bad thing as naïveté."

Valeant's History of Deal-Making

BY WILLIAM ALDEN | APRIL 21, 2014

VALEANT PHARMACEUTICALS, which said on Monday that it was teaming up with the hedge fund manager William A. Ackman to bid for the maker of Botox, is no stranger to deal-making.

The Canadian company, which was forged from the 2010 merger of Valeant and Biovail, is known as a serial acquirer, having spent billions of dollars on companies. Its latest, and biggest, target, Allergan, has a market value of about $42 billion.

Acquisitions are common in the world of health care, as companies seek control of lucrative new drugs, but Valeant has been among the most active. It has struck 30 deals since the Biovail transaction in 2010, according to Standard & Poor's Capital IQ.

The company has also engaged in prominent bids that have failed to result in deals. Below is a sampling of some of its deal-making activities.

SUCCESSES

Bausch & Lomb: Valeant agreed in May 2013 to buy the eye care company Bausch & Lomb for about $8.7 billion. The deal closed a few months later. Under its terms, Valeant paid $4.5 billion to the investors that owned Bausch & Lomb, led by the private equity firm Warburg Pincus, and spent about $4.2 billion to repay the company's debt.

Medicis: In September 2012, Valeant agreed to spend $2.6 billion for the Medicis Pharmaceutical Corporation, a skin care business based in Arizona. The deal closed that December.

Natur Produkt: The Medicis deal came during a particularly active year for Valeant. Among its acquisitions in 2012, it struck a $180 million deal for Natur Produkt International of Russia, a cough and cold pharmaceuticals provider.

FAILURES

Actavis: Merger talks between Valeant and another drug maker, Actavis, fell through in April 2013, a person briefed on the matter said at the time. Valeant might have paid more than $13 billion in stock to acquire the company. But not long after the collapse of the talks, Actavis agreed to buy a smaller rival, Warner Chilcott, for about $5 billion in stock.

Cephalon: Valeant unveiled a $5.7 billion hostile bid for Cephalon, a biopharmaceutical company, in March 2011. Cephalon rebuffed the offer as too low and opportunistic and, in May, it agreed to sell itself to Teva Pharmaceutical Industries for $6.8 billion.

Roche to Buy InterMune for $8.3 Billion

BY ANDREW POLLACK AND MICHAEL J. DE LA MERCED | AUG. 24, 2014

THE SWISS DRUG MAKER Roche agreed on Sunday to buy InterMune — which sells a drug to treat a deadly lung disease — for $8.3 billion, as pharmaceutical companies continue to seek new products to bolster their offerings.

The price, $74 a share, represents a 38 percent premium to InterMune's closing price on Friday and a 63 percent premium to the price on Aug. 12, before news reports that InterMune might be acquired.

The acquisition was announced during a flurry of pharmaceutical deals and attempted deals. About $87 billion in pharmaceutical acquisitions were made in the first half of this year, eclipsing the total for all of 2013, according to Evaluate, a research company. The total for the first half does not include the $54 billion acquisition of Shire by AbbVie, which was formally announced in July.

InterMune, based in Brisbane, Calif., has one product on the market: a drug called pirfenidone to treat idiopathic pulmonary fibrosis, a fatal scarring of the lungs.

InterMune, which is still not profitable, sells pirfenidone under the name Esbriet in Europe and Canada, where it received regulatory approval in 2011 and 2012. The drug could receive approval in the United States by Nov. 23.

Sales of Esbriet were $35.7 million in the second quarter, but some analysts expect annual revenues to eventually exceed $1 billion.

"We are obviously focused on high unmet medical needs and looking for medicines that make a significant difference clinically, and this clearly fits that bill," Daniel O'Day, who runs Roche's pharmaceutical business, said in an interview on Sunday.

He said the acquisition would strengthen its portfolio of drugs for respiratory diseases. That has not been a major business for a company mainly known for its cancer treatments. Roche sells Xolair, a drug for asthma, and Pulmozyme for cystic fibrosis. But it has another drug, lebrikizumab, that is in late-stage clinical trials to treat severe asthma and is also being evaluated as a possible treatment for idiopathic pulmonary fibrosis.

Roche, however, has historically not relied much on acquisitions for its pharmaceutical business, though it has in its diagnostics business. The big exception was its acquisition of the part of biotechnology pioneer Genentech that it did not already own for $46.8 billion in 2009.

In the last couple of months, Roche has announced some smaller acquisitions, agreeing to pay at least $725 million for privately held Seragon Pharmaceuticals, which is developing breast cancer drugs, and at least $250 million for privately held Santaris Pharma, which develops drugs that work by affecting RNA.

Idiopathic pulmonary fibrosis, which has no known cause, affects 70,000 to 200,000 Americans, according to various estimates. As scarring builds up in the lungs, people gradually lose the ability to breathe. Death often occurs two to five years after diagnosis.

No treatments are approved for use in the United States, though steroids and some other drugs are used off label, and a relatively small number of patients can receive lung transplants.

But Esbriet, if it is approved, probably will not have the market to itself for long because Boehringer Ingelheim of Germany has also applied for approval of a drug called nintedanib.

Both drugs slow the decline in lung function, according to papers in The New England Journal of Medicine in May. Evidence from clinical trials indicates that pirfenidone can also help patients live longer, though it is not clear if the evidence is strong enough for that to be listed on the drug's label if it is approved.

Mr. O'Day said data from the latest clinical trial, published in May, drew Roche's interest. He said his company approached InterMune in late July.

The acquisition represents a triumph for InterMune after a history of travails. A previous drug being tested for pulmonary fibrosis failed in clinical trials. The company's former chief executive, W. Scott Harkonen, was convicted of wire fraud for issuing a news release that prosecutors said was an effort to promote off-label sales of that drug. Then, in 2010 the Food and Drug Administration rejected pirfenidone, asking for an additional clinical trial.

The merger is expected to close by year end. Mr. O'Day declined to say if there would be layoffs, though he said the main purpose of the merger was "growth synergies."

Citigroup and the law firm Davis Polk & Wardwell advised Roche. Centerview Partners, Goldman Sachs and the law firm Cravath, Swaine & Moore advised InterMune.

Why Are So Few Blockbuster Drugs Invented Today?

BY DAN HURLEY | NOV. 13, 2014

IN THE FALL of 1999, a young chemical engineer named Todd Zion left his job at Eastman Kodak to enroll in the Ph.D. program at the Massachusetts Institute of Technology. While looking for a subject to research, Zion noticed a grant proposal, never funded, that another graduate student had written on the subject of drug delivery. One possibility mentioned in the proposal was the development of a kind of insulin that would automatically respond to changes in blood-sugar levels, becoming active only when needed to maintain healthy levels around the clock. If it worked, the sugar-sensitive version could transform the lives of the six million people with diabetes in the United States who use insulin. No longer would they have to test their blood-sugar levels multiple times per day and try to calculate how much insulin to take. The self-regulating insulin would curtail high sugar levels, which raise the risk of long-term complications, and eradicate, or at least reduce, the most dangerous short-term complication: hypoglycemia, when sugar levels fall so low that they can cause confusion, unconsciousness, seizures and even death.

"I thought, Wow, that is a really neat area in which to do research," Zion told me. Other researchers had been trying for 20 years to make insulin work only when needed. The first to publish a study were the scientists Michael Brownlee and Anthony Cerami, who in 1979 embedded a sugar-encrusted form of insulin in a mesh pouch with a sugar-loving protein called lectin. The idea was that when blood-sugar levels were elevated, the lectin would bind to the sugar in the blood and allow the insulin to leak out; when sugar levels were normal, the lectin would bind to the sugar-encrusted insulin, keeping it inside the pouch. But the system was impractical, because the pouch would need to be implanted under the skin and periodically refilled. And the lectin, derived from the jack-bean plant, was toxic.

In his first three years at M.I.T., Zion used nanoscale molecular engineering to create an insulin-lectin gel that could be injected without the need for an implanted pouch, while also rejiggering the lectin to make it less toxic. "It worked great visually," he said. When the gel was placed in a sugar solution, "you could see the outer edge getting clear and dissolving ... almost like an ice cube melting in water."

The problem was that, no matter how hard he tried to manipulate the gel, the insulin either leaked out too easily, even when sugar levels were low, or not easily enough, when sugar levels were high.

Zion knew there was another approach: changing the insulin molecule itself, to make it sensitive to blood-sugar levels directly. But, he said, "almost everyone in the field of drug discovery believed that you should never, ever change the insulin molecule. ... From a regulatory point of view, as soon as you manipulate the molecule, you've created a new drug. It doesn't matter if you've attached a single atom to it." Doing so, he knew, would require years of clinical trials in preparation for a new-drug application submission to the F.D.A. "That's the only reason people were afraid."

After three years of struggle and frustration at M.I.T., Zion figured he had no other choice. The big aha moment for him, he said, was when he realized he would have to take the step others feared. "I said the only way for this to be possible would be to chemically engineer the insulin itself. The result, yes, would be a new chemical entity, but it might actually work."

Zion's trick was to attach a chemical arm — a short chain of sugars — directly onto the insulin molecule. (Attaching sugar to insulin? "Yes, it is a bit ironic," he concedes.) The beauty of this approach is that it permits the insulin to latch directly onto the sugar-loving lectin in the gel — but only as needed. When blood-sugar levels are high, the lectin hooks up with any sugar floating freely from the blood, allowing the insulin molecule to do its normal job of connecting with insulin receptors on the surface of cells. (That is how insulin lowers blood-sugar levels, by merging with a cell's insulin receptor and unlocking the cell membrane to allow sugar in.) When the sugar gets swallowed up by cells, lowering levels in the blood, the only remaining sweet for the lectin to attach to is the altered insulin's sugar arm. Handcuffed to the lectin, the insulin can't bind to insulin receptors. And so the insulin stops working to lower blood-sugar levels precisely when it's no longer needed, because its sugar chain is held hostage by the lectin.

Zion called his new chemical creation smart insulin. In 2003, after testing it in rats, he won M.I.T.'s annual Entrepreneurship Competition. With the $30,000 prize money, he started a company called SmartCells and tried to see if he could make it work well enough to test it in humans.

The two biggest remaining problems were that the lectin-insulin gel was much bulkier than plain insulin alone, and that the lectin continued to produce minor, unwanted side effects. In 2008 Zion solved both when he figured out a way to tweak the sugar arm of his altered insulin molecule so it would bind with the type of lectin receptors already present on every cell in the body. Suddenly, he realized, there was no need to add the plant-based lectin in order for the drug to work.

The final version of his smart insulin was so promising that in December 2010, the drug company Merck, one of the largest in the world, announced it was buying SmartCells and its patents for what could eventually reach more than half a billion dollars, all for a drug that has yet to be taken by a single human being.

Should smart insulin eventually gain F.D.A. approval, its success would be more than a breakthrough in the treatment of diabetes, and certainly much more than a business win for Merck. For the pharmaceutical industry — which during the past two decades has increasingly focused on an automated, high-tech approach to discovering drugs — it would mark a victory for old-fashioned trial-and-error chemistry, the kind of endless tinkering and mucking around in the dark that by now was supposed to be a thing of the past.

ON SEPT. 25, 1990, James D. Watson, the Nobel Prize-winning co-discoverer of the double-helix structure of DNA, and at the time the director of the National Center for Human Genome Research, wrote a letter to this paper making a prediction: "The ability to sequence DNA quickly and cheaply will also provide the technological basis for a new era in drug development."

At that moment, the idea that the human genome would lead to a multitude of cures for diseases seemed inevitable and irresistible. DNA is, after all, nature's instruction booklet for building living things; open that book and read its instructions, the thinking ran, and the botched instructions that result in diseases would be revealed. From there, a logical series of steps would arrive at a cure. Once a malfunctioning gene was isolated, scientists would find the protein coded by that gene. Then they'd use that protein as a target. Finally, they'd run tests of tens of thousands of unique chemical entities that drug companies have stockpiled over the years, to find one that fit the target like a key in a lock, to correct its function.

But this golden road to pharmaceutical riches, known as target-based drug discovery, has often proved to be more of a garden path. The first disappointment has been that most diseases affecting large numbers of people are not caused by a handful of mutations that can be unearthed as easily as digging potatoes in a field. Geneticists have called this the problem of "missing heritability," because despite what they promised in the 1990s, they have found no single genetic variants that are necessary and sufficient to cause most forms of widespread diseases like diabetes, heart disease, Alzheimer's or cancer.

The second disappointment is that even when a genetic variation can be plainly linked to a disease, the process for figuring out what to do about it rarely works as efficiently as advertised. Compounds that appear to hit a designated target right between the eyes still often fail to be safe and effective in animal and human studies. Biology is just way too complicated.

"If you read them now, the claims made for genomics in the 1990s sound a bit like predictions made in the 1950s for flying cars and anti-gravity devices," Jack Scannell, an industry analyst, told me. But rather than speeding drug development, genomics may have slowed it down. So far it has produced fewer returns on greater investments. Scannell and Brian Warrington, who worked for 40 years inventing drugs for pharmaceutical companies, published a grim paper in 2012 that showed the plummeting efficiency of the pharmaceutical industry. They found that for every billion dollars spent on research and development since 1950, the number of new drugs approved has fallen by half roughly every nine years, meaning a total decline by a factor of 80. They called this Eroom's Law, because it resembled an inversion of Moore's Law (the observation, first made by the Intel co-founder Gorden E. Moore in 1965, that the number of transistors in an integrated circuit doubles approximately every two years).

That's not to say that target-based drug discovery, informed by genomics, hasn't had its share of spectacular successes. Gleevec, used since 2001 to treat chronic myelogenous leukemia (C.M.L.) and a variety of other cancers, is often pointed to as one of the great gene-to-medicine success stories. Its design followed logically from the identification of an abnormal protein caused by a genetic glitch found in almost every cancer cell of patients with C.M.L.

Many of the drugs developed through target-based discovery, however, work for only single mutation diseases affecting a tiny number of people. Seventy percent of new drugs approved by the F.D.A. last year were so-called specialty drugs used by no more than 1 percent of the population. The drug Kalydeco, for instance, was approved in 2012 for people with a particular genetic mutation that causes cystic fibrosis. But only about 1,200 people in the United States have the mutation it corrects. For them it can be a lifesaver, but for the tens of millions of people suffering from more widespread diseases, target-based drugs derived from genomics have offered little.

“We still have big public health needs,” said John Jenkins, director of the F.D.A.’s Office of New Drugs. “We’re hoping companies don’t lose track of the broader diseases, like diabetes, as they pursue genomic science and targeted therapies.”

So far, most drug companies have continued to devote a vast majority of their funding to target-based research, even as more traditional methods of drug discovery have proved more productive. A study published last year by David Swinney found that only 17 of 50 novel drugs approved by the F.D.A. between 1999 and 2008 came from target-based research, compared with 28 from what Swinney calls “phenotypic” discovery, made by studying living cells in Petri dishes, animals and humans. Many of the drugs in this latter category — Alamast for allergies, Amitiza for constipation, Abreva for herpes cold sores, Ranexa for angina, Veregen for genital warts and Keppra, Excegran and Inovelon for seizures — were discovered by chemists who didn’t set out knowing what the drugs’ targets were, or even how they worked. In one now well known case of nontargeted research, scientists developed a drug for angina and found that while it wasn’t effective for relieving chest pain, it did cause erections in the study’s male volunteers. The researchers changed course, and Viagra was born.

Swinney, chief executive of the Institute for Rare and Neglected Diseases Drug Discovery, spent the first 25 years of his career as a drug researcher, looking for the kind of targets that genomics was supposed to provide.

“I’ve done an about-face,” said Swinney, who estimates that more than 80 percent of research funding is still spent on target-based approaches. “The target-based research made possible by genomics is cool and fascinating,” he went on. But, he conceded, “you know what? We almost never use this information before we discover a drug. … This whole idea is too simplistic for the overall complexity of biology.”

Another veteran chemist, Derek Lowe, worked at Bayer when the genomics revolution was in full flourish. “The whole industry went crazy with it,” said Lowe, who writes In the Pipeline, a blog about the pharmaceutical industry. "Bayer committed half a billion dollars into human genome research, and they got nothing for it. Nothing at all."

OF COURSE, an overreliance on genomics is not the only factor slowing down the discovery of new drugs, as industry analysts are quick to point out. One challenge is that the industry is the victim of its own previous successes. In order to thrive, it must come up with drugs that work better than blockbusters of the past. After all, old drugs don't fade away; they just go generic. Scannell and Warrington have dubbed this the "Better Than the Beatles" problem, as if every new song in the recording industry had to be bigger than "Hey Jude" or "I Want to Hold Your Hand."

At the same time, the demand for proof of safety and efficacy, not only from the F.D.A. but also from trial lawyers and the public at large, is far higher than in years past. The days when drugs like the original insulin could be sold within a year of their discovery by chemists are long gone, and rightly so.

To check the industry's slide, experts say that drug companies need to begin applying the new molecular engineering tools to old-fashioned methods of discovery. It may sound absurd to describe the newfangled nanoengineering that Zion used to develop smart insulin as "old-fashioned," but his fundamental approach is one that researchers from the 1950s would recognize. It is inductive, beginning with a close observation of chemicals and their behaviors in living systems, to then making tentative hypotheses and then going through a long tinkering process of trial and error to find something that works. The spirit that animates the trial-and-error chemists is an enthusiasm for constructing new drugs piece by molecular piece, like children playing with building blocks.

Brian Warrington, who retired in 2005 as Britain's vice president of discovery technology development at GlaxoSmithKline UK, says that creating new drugs through trial and error was a thing of joy. "You're just watching something happening in a chemical reaction," he told me, "and then realizing, Wait a minute, that went strangely. I wonder why."

Warrington told me about his late colleague Sir James Black, a Nobel Prize-winning pharmacologist, who was one of the great practitioners of trial-and-error discovery. In the early 1960s, he developed propranolol, the first beta blocker for heart disease, which for a while was the world's best-selling drug. Then he developed the first H2-receptor antagonist for treating peptic ulcers, cimetidine, which took the top-selling spot from propranolol in the 1970s. "He developed some of the greatest drugs of the 20th century by looking at phenomena and asking the right questions," Warrington said. "He didn't need the genome."

The progress of smart insulin has not been as fast as some might have hoped since it was acquired by Merck. The company declined to let me talk to its scientists, but it announced in May that it planned to begin testing the drug, which it calls L-490, in humans by the end of this year. Assuming a typical six-year timetable from the beginning of the first Phase 1 trial to the completion of a large Phase 3 trial, plus another year for F.D.A. review, it would be 2021 at the earliest before people whose diabetes requires treatment with insulin would be able to get the smart kind — more than two decades after Zion began working on it.

Zion says he is grateful to know that his drug is one step closer to making it out into the world, and not just because it could help millions of people. He also sees it as a validation of the idea that the attempt-and-fail model can produce something marvelous. "It's really engineering," Zion said. "You have to become the master of something no one ever knew existed before."

$2.6 Billion to Develop a Drug? New Estimate Makes Questionable Assumptions

BY AARON E. CARROLL | NOV. 18, 2014

THE TUFTS CENTER for the Study of Drug Development has just released its newest estimate for the cost to develop and bring a drug to market. At $2.6 billion, this figure is bound to get a lot of attention. We should take this announcement with a grain of salt, however. While it is no doubt expensive to create a drug, such announcements have come under attack before, often with good reason.

The Tufts Center is funded, to a large extent, by the pharmaceutical industry. It is in the pharmaceutical industry's best interests to have the public believe that it is very expensive to develop a drug. This belief helps drug companies justify the high prices they often charge. As I've said before here at The Upshot, financial conflicts of interest can have a great deal of influence, and we would be remiss to ignore them in this case.

But let's talk about the particulars of how the number $2.6 billion was calculated. The truth is, I can't give you as nearly as much detail as I'd like. That's because the study itself has not been published or peer reviewed. There are a news release, a set of slides and a backgrounder that describe the overview, but not as much detail as you'd see in a journal.

This is what happened in 2001, as well, when the Tufts Center released its finding that drugs took an average of $800 million to develop ($1 billion in 2013 dollars, the year used for the current study, the center said). The paper that summarized the methods by which they arrived at that number was published more than a year later, in 2003.

After those detailed methods were published, a number of people took exception to them. It might be helpful to review the concerns from last time in light of this latest announcement.

In both of these announcements, a significant amount of the costs to develop the drugs were opportunity, or time, costs. They are the returns that might be expected, but that investors went without, while a drug was in development. When a drug company invests in research and development, it is tying up money that could otherwise be invested elsewhere. In this announcement, the Tufts Center says that $1.2 billion of the $2.6 billion is time costs.

In other words, they estimate that drug companies could have made more money if they used their research investment for things other than drug development. While this is a perfectly sound economic argument, it often rings false to many. It's true that a drug company might have been able to make more money by increasing spending in the short term on marketing, or by investing in land, but if at some point it doesn't invest in research and development, it won't be a drug company anymore.

Moving on, that leaves an out-of-pocket cost of $1.4 billion for drug development. That's still a lot of money. But, assuming that the Tufts Center used a methodology similar to the one it used last time, it made some assumptions that are questionable.

The Food and Drug Administration considers some drugs to be new molecular entities, or N.M.E.s. These are drugs that contain active ingredients that have not been approved for individual use or as part of combination therapies in the past. It makes sense that the research and development for an N.M.E. would be higher than for other drugs. But N.M.E.s represent only a relatively small percentage of drugs approved each year by the F.D.A.; many more are "copycat drugs," slightly different versions of drugs already on the market. These, it's fair to assume, are much less expensive to develop.

Another issue concerns who paid for the research. A fairly large amount of research is funded by the public through the National Institutes of Health and other entities. Sometimes, this research later leads to drug development. For those drugs, and they have constituted a significant percentage of important drugs, the pharmaceutical industry did not bear all of the costs of research.

But in its last study, and, apparently, in this study, the Tufts Center considered only drugs that were new molecular entities and were developed entirely in-house by pharmaceutical companies. There's no question that these would be the most expensive drugs developed by those companies. However, they represent a minority of drugs, and they're certainly not "average." Yet those were the only drugs used to calculate the "average" cost.

Moreover, it appears that all of the data for the drugs were provided by the pharmaceutical companies themselves. Those data are secret, and no one else gets to really see or verify them. This creates a large potential for conflict of interest. Although the Tufts study said that the drugs it considered were randomly selected from the companies' portfolios, there's no independent proof of that.

Finally, it's worth mentioning that the research costs of drugs to pharmaceutical companies are tax deductible. That doesn't mean those costs aren't real, but it does mean that part of them are already being covered by taxpayers as a tax expenditure.

In an email late Wednesday, Joseph A. DiMasi, the lead author of the study, said that N.I.H. and other public research funding was "just part of the social cost of drug development" and irrelevant to what he was trying to measure, which was what private companies spend. He said the researchers did not exclude drugs from the study on the basis that they may have been developed using underlying knowledge funded by the N.I.H.

Mr. DiMasi said the other comments I've made on the study were similar to what he called the "wrong-headed methodological criticisms" raised at the time of the earlier work, which the researchers had responded to in a separate paper.

The bottom line is that the report contains a lot of assumptions that tend to favor the pharmaceutical industry. While the Tufts Center reports that $2.6 billion is the cost to develop "a new prescription medicine that gains marketing approval," it might be more accurate to say that it's the cost to develop certain new molecular entities for which pharmaceutical companies did all of the research. That's very few drugs, in the scheme of things.

When the last study was published, a number of other organizations did their own analyses as well. One was by Public Citizen, the advocacy group founded by Ralph Nader, which basically took the amount that pharmaceutical companies reported in research and development over a period of time, and then divided it by the number of drugs that obtained F.D.A. approval. The group came up with $161 million.

In 2010, a systematic review of studies that looked at the cost of drug development was published in Health Policy. The review found 13 articles, with estimates ranging from $161 million to $1.8 billion (in 2009 dollars). Obviously, methodology matters.

The best thing might be for pharmaceutical companies to open their books and allow researchers to verify these findings independently. That's unlikely to occur. As long as others control the data and the methods used to analyze them, we will continue to disagree as to how much it costs to develop new drugs.

Stop Subsidizing Big Pharma

OPINION | BY LLEWELLYN HINKES-JONES | JAN. 5, 2015

WASHINGTON — Robert J. Beall, the president and chief executive of the Cystic Fibrosis Foundation, called his recent decision to sell the royalty rights to his organization's research a "game changer." Indeed, deals like this, in which an investment company paid the foundation $3.3 billion for its future royalties from several cystic fibrosis drugs it helped finance, could revolutionize the way medical research is funded. Rather than the staid model of government-funded institutions handing out grants to academic research facilities, a new breed of "venture philanthropies" like the Cystic Fibrosis Foundation could corral private investment into developing lifesaving drugs quickly and cheaply.

The problem is that venture philanthropy is, essentially, another term for privatizing scientific research. Instead of decisions about the fate of scientific funding being made by publicly oriented institutions, those decisions are being put in the hands of anonymous philanthropists and ostensibly benevolent nonprofits.

At the risk of oversimplification, biomedical research divides into two categories: private and public. The former is the constellation of big pharmaceutical companies and start-up labs. The latter comprises government agencies and the universities and philanthropies that rely on government support — directly, through grants, or indirectly, through tax policy. The former can charge whatever it wants for its products; the latter is limited by government rules and price controls.

Venture philanthropy complicates this picture by introducing a tax-exempt loophole. An organization like the Cystic Fibrosis Foundation will take in tax-exempt donations to invest in a pharmaceutical company — in this case, Vertex Pharmaceuticals — to develop drugs based on publicly funded research. Venture philanthropies can then sell the results of that research to private industry to deliver drugs to the market.

YEHTEH

There is nothing to stop pharmaceutical companies from creating their own philanthropies, funding research with tax-exempt dollars and then selling themselves the rights to the intellectual property. Without price controls on the final product that come with public funding, the potential costs of the resulting medicines are limitless.

So far, there is no effort to extend government price controls to venture-philanthropy-derived research. The Cystic Fibrosis Foundation did little to lobby for lower prices on the drugs that were developed from the research it funded. As a result, Kalydeco, a cystic fibrosis medication it funded, is one of the most expensive drugs available, at $300,000 a year.

The idea of a public-private research transfer is not without precedent. In 1980, Congress passed the Bayh-Dole Act, which allowed publicly funded universities to sell off exclusive licenses on their research to private industry. The act was intended to drive funding for academic research and innovation.

But the resulting race for private funding has created perverse incentives to research blockbuster drugs, even if they are not the most imperative from a public policy standpoint. The impetus to produce more and more profitable research has also driven down the quality of academic work, promoting ghostwritten papers, sloppy peer review and the burying of unfavorable clinical-trial results. Venture philanthropy builds off the model created by Bayh-Dole, but with tax exemptions and a sheen of generosity on top of the lucrative payoff.

One argument in favor of venture philanthropy is that it creates a way to sustain small foundations that study rare diseases that, from a for-profit point of view, aren't worth investigating.

But while Big Pharma might be faulted for funneling billions of dollars into erectile-dysfunction drugs and off-label drug marketing, researching extremely rare diseases may also represent a misuse of public and private funds. Efforts to cure, rather than treat or prevent, obscure diseases can be expensive, diverting investment from more common afflictions. The high costs of focusing on rare diseases are then eventually pushed onto the health care system by way of egregiously high drug prices. Such a choice involves an incredibly complex moral calculus, one that is best processed by democratic public institutions.

To make medical advancements truly philanthropic, the profit motive needs to be removed from the equation. If the intent is to cure rare diseases, then we should be increasing the budget for the National Institutes of Health and other research initiatives. Instead of gala balls and donor drives, higher taxes on the same rich benefactors could be used to fund the research that isn't already being supported. Biotech patents developed through venture philanthropy should not have exclusive rights attached to them.

This would allow generic versions of drugs onto the market, which would go a long way toward keeping health care costs down and not driving the uninsured into debt.

LLEWELLYN HINKES-JONES is a journalist.

Ways to Fund Research on Rare Diseases

LETTER | THE NEW YORK TIMES | JAN. 12, 2015

TO THE EDITOR:

RE "STOP SUBSIDIZING Big Pharma," by Llewellyn Hinkes-Jones (Op-Ed, Jan. 5):

The Cystic Fibrosis Foundation is working tirelessly for people suffering from this fatal genetic disease. Sixty years ago, when the foundation was established, the average life expectancy of a child with cystic fibrosis was five years. Today, because of innovative new treatments, average life expectancy is 41 years.

Without the foundation's venture philanthropy approach, this progress would simply not have happened.

By investing in early-stage research, we ensure that people who suffer from this rare disease are not left out in the cold waiting until those in government and industry decide to address the urgent need for cystic fibrosis treatments.

Nearly every cystic fibrosis drug available today exists because of our support. Because of the tremendous advancements in research and care, many people with cystic fibrosis are now going to college, embarking on careers and having families of their own — living lives they could not have imagined just a short time ago.

In all we do, our sole commitment is to people with cystic fibrosis; our only "return" is in the tomorrows we add to their lives. Any funds generated from our research investments are plowed directly back into new research to find a cure and improve the health and quality of life of people with the disease.

We are concerned about the high price of cystic fibrosis drugs, which we know place a burden on patients and families and are unsustainable for the health care system over all. We're committed to finding the balance between fostering new treatments and ensuring that cost is not a barrier to people with cystic fibrosis.

ROBERT J. BEALL
President and Chief Executive
Cystic Fibrosis Foundation
Bethesda, Md., Jan. 7, 2015

TO THE EDITOR:

It seems that the privatization of medical discoveries is anathema to Llewellyn Hinkes-Jones, but the privatization of research is as American as apple pie, Model T's and light bulbs. Over time, the contribution to "public science" from agencies like the National Institutes of Health has decreased (only about 15 percent of grant applications receive funding). Where does he think the new medicines are going to come from?

If the tax laws need some adjusting so investors aren't using tax-exempt organizations as vehicles for tax-free investment, that's reasonable. Putting any restrictions on Big Pharma to invest and discover and profit from both is unreasonable.

Now if you want to clamp down, do so on the academic side, where putatively dispassionate investigators are taking money from companies to do research, the results of which, if successful (and true), will line their own pockets in the form of stock, travel and free food from their industry sponsors.

The wall between public and private research should be a high one, but there should be aggressive activity on both sides of this green line.

LEONARD ZWELLING
Bellaire, Tex., Jan. 6, 2015
The writer is an oncologist.

AstraZeneca to Acquire Majority Stake in Acerta Pharma

BY CHAD BRAY | DEC. 17, 2015

LONDON — The British drug maker AstraZeneca said on Thursday that it had agreed to acquire a majority stake in Acerta Pharma, a privately-held cancer drug developer with operations in the Netherlands and in California, for $4 billion.

The deal gives AstraZeneca the option to buy the remainder of the company for $3 billion more and would further bolster its line of cancer treatments.

Transactions in the health care sector have helped make 2015 a record year for global mergers and acquisitions.

Drug makers have used mergers and strategic investments to acquire promising treatments in late-stage development, hoping to claim the next blockbuster.

"The investment is consistent with our focus on long-term growth and reflects the role targeted business development plays in our business model," Pascal Soriot, the AstraZeneca chief executive, said in a news release about the Acerta Pharma deal.

"We are boosting a key area in our comprehensive oncology portfolio with a late-stage, potential best-in-class medicine that could transform treatment for patients across a range of blood cancers," he added.

Under the terms of the deal, AstraZeneca would acquire a 55 percent stake in Acerta for an initial payment of $2.5 billion. It would then pay $1.5 billion when acalabrutinib, Acerta's treatment for blood cancer, receives regulatory approval in the United States or by the end of 2018.

It would then have the option to buy the remainder of the company after the approval of the drug in Europe and the United States, and other milestones.

AstraZeneca said that an extensive development program for acalabrutinib was underway and that it might be able to take the first steps toward regulatory approval of treating patients with certain types of blood cancer in the second half of 2016.

The top yearly sales of the drug could exceed $5 billion globally, AstraZeneca said.

AstraZeneca announced on Monday that the companies were exploring “potential strategic options.”

AstraZeneca has said it would target similar small or midsize deals as it looks to bolster its drug pipeline after it fought off a $119 billion takeover bid by Pfizer last year, which would have created the world’s largest pharmaceutical company.

In November, AstraZeneca agreed to acquire ZS Pharma, a California-based biopharmaceutical company, for $2.7 billion in cash. This week, AstraZeneca also announced that it would acquire the core respiratory business of the Takeda Pharmaceutical Company of Japan for $575 million.

Explaining Valeant: The Main Theories

BY STEVEN DAVIDOFF SOLOMON | MARCH 29, 2016

WHETHER EXPERIENCING schadenfreude or finding insight, many think they know what is responsible for the turmoil at Valeant Pharmaceuticals International as it falls from a darling of Wall Street to its punching bag.

Commentators and analysts have drawn lessons, but few of them are convincing and many seem similar to the kinds of snap judgments that led to this mess.

Let's review the various explanations for Valeant's woes:

VALEANT AS ENRON

This argument contends that Valeant is a house of cards waiting to be brought down by an inevitable accounting scandal. When the debate over Valeant's accounting of its ties with the mail-order pharmacy Philidor Rx Services first began to rage, a report last October by the short seller Citron Research fanned the flames by comparing Valeant to Enron.

The Valeant-as-Enron theory was given a boost after Valeant failed to file its annual report on time because of an accounting restatement and after the board accused the company's former chief financial officer, Howard B. Schiller, of engaging in "improper conduct." For his part, Mr. Schiller says he has done nothing wrong.

The Enron theory is seductive, but Valeant is a real operating business that by all accounts is profitable. Unlike Enron, Valeant is not using accounting to cover up huge and unsustainable losses. Indeed, so far the accounting restatements have amounted to only $58 million worth of revenue. And while there may be more accounting restatements on the horizon, there is no indication of outright fraud.

BEWARE MCKINSEY

This view has gained traction in recent weeks. Valeant's chief executive,

J. Michael Pearson, is a former consultant at McKinsey, having spent 23 years there. And he apparently surrounded himself with former McKinsey people on his team.

So did Valeant's problems arise from a McKinsey-driven ethos devoted to driving shareholder value through financial machinations? Arguably, in the name of these McKinsey principles, Valeant was moved to Canada, shut down large portions of its research and development operations and became a vacuum swallowing up other pharmaceutical companies, all key to its growth strategy.

The McKinsey theory has surface appeal — after all, it is easy to make fun of consultants and their PowerPoint presentations. But McKinsey executives have also been at the forefront of arguments about long-term shareholder value and more disciplined acquisition policies. Elsewhere, McKinsey has formed an entire initiative on investing in long-term capital.

For good or bad, McKinsey advises thousands of companies, including many drug companies that do not engage in Valeant's business strategy.

THE PERILS OF R.&D. CUTS

This argument asserts that Valeant's business choices are coming home to roost. Valeant built itself on spending a reduced amount on research and development. Instead, it paid to acquire drugs and in some cases built profits by raising prices. This business strategy created its downfall — by failing to focus on developing drugs, Valeant left itself exposed to failure.

The foundation of this theory is the nonsensical notion that research and development can never be bad. Many drug companies, however, have been unable to capitalize on billions of dollars in research and development and are now resorting to purchases. Gilead Sciences, for example, made itself into a $100 billion company largely through the acquisition of a hepatitis C drug.

Shareholder activists are currently taking aim at technology companies for excessive spending on research and development without results. Not focusing on R.&D. was part of Valeant's business model, but that was not necessarily a problem in today's world. Indeed it made economic sense for Valeant. The company focused on sales and pricing — something at which it excelled, at least for a while — while others did the development.

PREDATORY PRICING

This view, made popular amid the uproar over Martin Shkreli, has a feel-good nature to it. Proponents of this theory focus on the fact that part of Valeant's business strategy was to buy drugs and sharply raise the prices. Now, with congressional scrutiny and other attacks, Valeant has backed away from this approach. The halt to this pricing strategy would seem to explain Valeant's decline.

The first problem with this theory is that we don't have transparency around Valeant's pricing, or indeed that of any pharmaceutical company. Valeant's headline price increases were most likely fought by insurers, and the actual increases were no doubt reduced in those battles.

It is clear that to the extent Valeant's expansion strategy relied on increasing prices, that is no longer a viable road to growth. But that does not mean there should be a sudden collapse of Valeant. After all, the drugs in its current stable of products are priced where they are and still sell.

THE HEDGE FUNDS

In this scenario, the blame lies with the shareholder activist fund ValueAct, which partly created the modern-day Valeant. ValueAct arranged for the hiring of Mr. Pearson and participated in creating a compensation package, which, including his stock and options, was worth at one point as much as $3 billion.

ValueAct also pressed Valeant to focus on cutting research and development (something that the fund also pushed at Microsoft) and use acquisitions as a substitute. For a time, this was an extraordinarily successful strategy. Even now, ValueAct is still in the black on the Valeant investment.

The problem with targeting ValueAct is that this explains the business strategy, but it does not help us understand what went wrong.

THE SHAREHOLDERS

There is certainly blame all around for the hedge funds that bid up Valeant's stock price. The Sequoia Fund, for example, inexplicably put more than a quarter of its portfolio into Valeant. (In a you-can't-make-this-up sidelight, Sequoia's chairman is Roger Lowenstein, the author of "When Genius Failed," about the collapse of Long-Term Capital Management.)

These investors should have known better than to chase returns, but this again has nothing to do with Valeant's business.

THE DEAL PROFESSOR THEORY

It is clear there are problems at Valeant, but if Wall Street built Valeant, it is now running away from it. And the velocity of the turnaround has distorted all views of the company. It has created a volatility untethered by reality. In the Wall Street worldview, Valeant is worth either zero or it is worth $100 a share.

But Valeant is a real company. It does not make sense for a company with earnings before interest, taxes, depreciation and amortization, or Ebitda, of about $5 billion a year to be worth only $9 billion. A rival drug company, Allergan, for example, with Ebitda of $7 billion a year and $40 billion of debt, is worth $110 billion.

To be sure, Valeant has about $30 billion in debt upon which it might technically default if it cannot file its annual financial statement by April 29. But such a situation is not that uncommon. Companies typically pay a fee to the banks and get a waiver from the debtholders.

There is no doubt that Valeant has taken a major hit. The crisis has crushed its previous business model of raising prices and making acquisitions. This has left it a company in transition. Valeant may still take some wrong steps, but wherever it goes from here, one can't ignore the business it already has — with billions of dollars in earnings.

The intrinsic worth of that business remains essentially the same. It is the company that is suffering from a crisis of confidence. The flight by Wall Street shut down Valeant's old business growth model, not its business.

But understanding requires thinking that is a bit too clear-eyed for Wall Street, which when things go bad, prefers the worst. And sometimes it creates a self-fulfilling frenzy. Remember the financial crisis, after all.

CHAPTER 2

Monopolies and Exclusivity Drive Price Spikes

With its new business model, drug manufacturers began cornering specific drug markets. Pharmaceutical companies acquired and held onto exclusive drugs in specific therapeutic areas; for example, respiratory disorders or rare diseases. Thus, they have been able to raise the prices for those drugs without competition, leaving people with no choice but to use their drugs. This chapter covers the issue of runaway drug prices and the risks of therapeutic monopolies. It also shows examples of how companies or individuals can take advantage of the sick.

Runaway Drug Prices

EDITORIAL | BY THE NEW YORK TIMES | MAY 5, 2015

A DRUG TO TREAT abnormal heart rhythms can cost about $200 on one day and more than $1,300 the next. A diagnosis of multiple sclerosis can lead to a drug bill of at least $50,000 a year. How companies set prices of specialty drugs for these and other complex diseases, like cancer and AIDS, has been a mystery to the patients who need them. Now the Obama administration and some states are tackling that lack of transparency and the rising costs.

Mr. Obama has asked Congress to let Medicare officials negotiate prices with drug manufacturers, a practice forbidden by current law that may be hard to change with the antiregulatory mood among Republicans. And several states are considering bills that would require drug companies to justify their prices to public agencies. It is the least the states can do to bring costs to levels that patients, hospitals and government programs can afford.

Spending on all prescription drugs, including commonly used medicines like antibiotics, accounts for a tenth of the nation's total health spending. Prices have been rising slowly in recent years mainly because many brand-name drugs lost protection and lower-cost generics were prescribed. But there are fewer patent expirations ahead. Specialized medicines already on the market carry huge price tags, as The Times reported recently, and strain the budgets of Medicare, Medicaid and consumers. The list price for a one-year's supply of Kalydeco to treat cystic fibrosis is $311,000. A standard course of treatment with Blincyto, a leukemia drug, is about $178,000.

Drugs used to treat multiple sclerosis are of particular concern. A recent study by researchers in Oregon found that first-generation drugs that came on the market in the 1990s ranged in price from $8,000 to $11,000 a year. Prices for those drugs rose even though new drugs entered the market, theoretically providing competition. One drug that first cost $8,700 now costs $62,400 a year.

There are no multiple sclerosis drugs available in the United States with a list price below $50,000 a year, the researchers say, which is two to three times more than the list prices in Canada, Australia or Britain.

The drug and biotech companies contend that high prices are justified to cover the large costs of bringing a drug to market and to compensate for the large number of drugs that fail in late stages of costly clinical trials. But it appears that many companies raise prices arbitrarily and charge what public and private insurers will pay.

A recent report in The Wall Street Journal described how Valeant Pharmaceuticals International, based in Canada, bought the rights to two lifesaving heart drugs on Feb. 10 and raised their prices the same day. The list price for a one-milliliter vial of Isuprel, used to treat abnormal heart rhythms, rose to $1,347 from $215. The price for a two-milliliter vial of Nitropress, for dangerously high blood pressure and acute heart failure, increased to $806 from $258. The Journal cites similar increases for Ofirmev pain injections and Vimovo pain tablets after new companies acquired the rights.

Bills have been introduced in several states requiring drug makers to report profits and expenses for costly drugs or sometimes for all drugs, according to The Journal's pharmaceutical blog. Such disclosures might shame companies into restraining their price increases and provide state officials with information to determine what action to take.

The industry helped defeat such a bill in Oregon and is fighting to head off a bill in California that would impose new reporting requirements on makers of any prescription drug whose wholesale costs are $10,000 or more annually or per course of treatment. They would have to disclose the research, development, marketing and manufacturing costs, as well as the profits, attributable to the drug. The companies complain that some of these costs are hard to quantify and that compiling the data would be burdensome. But surely the public would benefit from increased transparency that might deter the worst abuses.

Costly Hepatitis C Drugs for Everyone?

EDITORIAL | BY THE NEW YORK TIMES | SEPT. 2, 2015

NEW DRUGS TO TREAT hepatitis C are tremendously effective — and tremendously costly — raising fears that the high prices might outstrip the ability of public and private insurers to pay. Fortunately, competitive market forces and hard-nosed bargaining by insurers for big discounts are going a long way toward resolving the problem.

The drugs are sorely needed. The hepatitis C virus caused nearly 20,000 deaths in the United States in 2013, many in patients who were also infected with H.I.V., the human immunodeficiency virus that causes AIDS, a double whammy that triples their risk of liver disease.

There are four new drugs approved to treat hepatitis C: Sovaldi and Harvoni, made by Gilead Sciences; Viekira Pak, made by AbbVie; and Daklinza, made by Bristol-Myers Squibb. The cost for Sovaldi is $84,000 for a standard 12-week course of treatment, which breaks down to about $1,000 for each pill, taken daily. State Medicaid programs typically obtain discounts, but prices still generally exceed $600 a pill. Harvoni is even more expensive, with a list price of about $95,000 for a 12-week course of treatment without a discount.

The benefits of these new drugs are undeniable. They can essentially cure the infection in eight to 24 weeks. Older medications are not nearly as effective and often produce disabling side effects. Curing the patient decreases by more than 80 percent the risk of liver cancer, liver failure and the need for a liver transplant, thus saving money in the long run. Successful treatment can also greatly reduce the number of new cases of hepatitis C by preventing transmission of the virus through needle-sharing among drug addicts infected with H.I.V.

After Gilead announced this year that it would give an average discount of 46 percent off the list prices of its two drugs, the Institute for Clinical and Economic Review, previously a skeptic, estimated that a likely course of treatment with Harvoni would make it a high value for individual patients and for most health care systems.

Unfortunately, most state Medicaid programs, in an effort to control costs, have placed restrictions on making the drugs widely available. These include requiring that patients have advanced liver disease before they can get the drug, requiring patients to abstain from alcohol or illicit drugs for at least a year before treatment, and requiring that the drugs be prescribed only by specialists like infectious disease experts or gastroenterologists.

The restrictions run counter to guidelines published by the Infectious Diseases Society of America and the American Association for the Study of Liver Diseases, which recommend treating all patients infected with the hepatitis C virus except those who have a life expectancy of less than a year because of some other disease. A June 9 letter to President Obama from the Presidential Advisory Council on H.I.V./AIDS called for eliminating such "unreasonable" restrictions. It said that increased competition had "dramatically reduced" the cost of treatment.

Even so, there is probably room to drive prices down even further. With these and other high-priced drugs, the manufacturers typically charge what the market will bear. The public and private insurers that pay for hepatitis C drugs should press for even bigger discounts.

New Cholesterol Drugs Are Vastly Overpriced, Analysis Says

BY ANDREW POLLACK | SEPT. 8, 2015

TWO POWERFUL NEW DRUGS that can sharply lower cholesterol are vastly overpriced based on the value they provide, according to a new analysis by an independent organization that evaluates pharmaceutical costs.

The analysis, released on Tuesday, said that measured by the health benefits the drugs provide, the price should be only about one-third the level set by the manufacturers. The cost should be even lower — about 15 percent of list price — to avoid straining health care budgets, it said.

The new report is from the Institute for Clinical and Economic Review, a nonprofit organization that made a name for itself last year when it warned about the costs of new drugs to treat hepatitis C.

Health plans use the group's reports, and this new one could increase pressure on the makers of the cholesterol drugs to offer bigger discounts. Express Scripts, the country's largest pharmaceutical benefit manager, has said it plans to use the report's findings in its negotiations with the drug companies.

The two drugs, Repatha from Amgen and Praluent from Sanofi and Regeneron Pharmaceuticals, were approved by the Food and Drug Administration in the last two months. In clinical trials they lowered the level of LDL cholesterol, the so-called bad kind, by 40 percent or more, even when patients were already taking statins.

But the drugs' prices — $14,100 a year for Repatha and $14,600 a year for Praluent — have raised concern about costs, especially since the drugs might be used year after year by millions of Americans.

"Even if these drugs were used in just over 25 percent of eligible patients, then employers, insurers and patients would need to spend on average more than $20 billion a year," Dr. Steven D. Pearson, the founder and president of ICER, said in a statement.

The analysis said the drugs should cost $3,615 to $4,811 a year, based on the value they are expected to provide in terms of preventing heart attacks and deaths.

The drugs should cost even less — $2,177 — the analysis said, to be at a level where health plans would not have to limit their use to prevent straining health care budgets.

ICER's report is expected to be the first of many, from different organizations and academic researchers, to assess the cost-effectiveness of the cholesterol drugs, and some may reach different conclusions since much depends on the assumptions used. ICER termed its report a draft that would be open to public comment and discussed at a meeting in Boston on Oct. 27.

Amgen said in a statement on Tuesday that while it welcomed a "balanced discussion of value," it disagreed with ICER's methodology, assumptions and preliminary conclusions, which it noted had not undergone public comment or formal peer review.

"We are concerned that ICER's review does not place value on addressing a significant unmet medical need," the statement said, "and its short-term budgetary focus will be used to create access barriers to innovative medicines like Repatha for appropriate patients."

Regeneron said it had not had adequate time to review ICER's report. But a spokeswoman said, "These calculations are complex, and a robust and open peer-review process is essential."

One big potential problem with the analysis is that it is not known whether the drugs prevent heart attacks, strokes or death, and if they do, by how much. Large clinical trials aimed at answering those questions are expected to have results around 2017.

But ICER estimated the potential benefits on the basis of an amalgamation of results from smaller trials and on the level of cholesterol reduction achieved by the drugs. It said that use of the drugs might reduce mortality from all causes by about 50 percent.

The organization applied those benefits to a computer simulation of the adult American population, tallying up the costs of the drugs as well as potential cost savings, such as those from reduced hospitalizations for heart attacks.

It estimated that use of the drugs would prevent hundreds of thousands of deaths, heart attacks or strokes over the next 20 years, but at a cost exceeding $500,000 for each additional "quality-adjusted life-year."

That is a measure used by health economists, in which a year of life in perfect health is one quality-adjusted life-year, while a year in less than good health is some fraction of a life-year.

Health care economists use different thresholds for determining when a procedure or drug is cost-effective. Some say less than $50,000 per quality-adjusted life-year; others say less than $100,000 or less than $150,000. To get to the $150,000 level, the cholesterol drugs would have to cost $4,811 a year, and to get to $100,000, they would have to cost $3,615, according to the analysis.

Dr. Troyen Brennan, chief medical officer of CVS Health, a pharmacy benefit manager, said ICER's conclusions were "basically right in line with our view of the medications — that they have some value, but at their current prices they are way overpriced."

Inflated Drug Prices

LETTER | THE NEW YORK TIMES | SEPT. 14, 2015

TO THE EDITOR:

AS THE COUNTRY grapples with the staggering cost of new hepatitis C medications, we agree that more needs to be done to lower drug prices. Your Sept. 2 editorial "Costly Hepatitis C Drugs for Everyone?" urges the type of market-based solutions that will benefit patients and promote innovation. But we should not assume that the five- and six-figure launch prices for these drugs are reasonable and appropriate.

Drug makers' monopoly pricing power gives little incentive for these companies to price at a responsible — let alone sustainable — level. Case in point: Pharmasset, the company that developed Sovaldi, planned an initial launch price around $36,000 for a 12-week course of treatment. That's less than half of what Gilead Sciences charged when the drug came to market. As a result, health plans were forced to negotiate at an inflated price level for Sovaldi and every other hepatitis C drug. That's not a sign of competition; that's exploitation.

Health plans negotiate every day to get the best price for patients, but improving access to affordable medications requires greater transparency around pricing and value so that a truly informed negotiation can happen. All players in the health system must embrace the goals of affordability. Pharmaceutical companies need to get on board.

DAN DURHAM
Executive Vice President
America's Health Insurance Plans
Washington

Drug Goes From $13.50 a Tablet to $750, Overnight

BY ANDREW POLLACK | SEPT. 20, 2015

SPECIALISTS IN INFECTIOUS disease are protesting a gigantic overnight increase in the price of a 62-year-old drug that is the standard of care for treating a life-threatening parasitic infection.

The drug, called Daraprim, was acquired in August by Turing Pharmaceuticals, a start-up run by a former hedge fund manager. Turing immediately raised the price to $750 a tablet from $13.50, bringing the annual cost of treatment for some patients to hundreds of thousands of dollars.

"What is it that they are doing differently that has led to this dramatic increase?" said Dr. Judith Aberg, the chief of the division of infectious diseases at the Icahn School of Medicine at Mount Sinai. She said the price increase could force hospitals to use "alternative therapies that may not have the same efficacy."

Turing's price increase is not an isolated example. While most of the attention on pharmaceutical prices has been on new drugs for diseases like cancer, hepatitis C and high cholesterol, there is also growing concern about huge price increases on older drugs, some of them generic, that have long been mainstays of treatment.

Although some price increases have been caused by shortages, others have resulted from a business strategy of buying old neglected drugs and turning them into high-priced "specialty drugs."

Cycloserine, a drug used to treat dangerous multidrug-resistant tuberculosis, was just increased in price to $10,800 for 30 pills from $500 after its acquisition by Rodelis Therapeutics. Scott Spencer, general manager of Rodelis, said the company needed to invest to make sure the supply of the drug remained reliable. He said the company provided the drug free to certain needy patients.

In August, two members of Congress investigating generic drug price increases wrote to Valeant Pharmaceuticals after that company acquired two heart drugs, Isuprel and Nitropress, from Marathon Pharmaceuticals and promptly raised their prices by 525 percent and 212 percent respectively. Marathon had acquired the drugs from another company in 2013 and had quintupled their prices, according to the lawmakers, Senator Bernie Sanders, the Vermont independent who is seeking the Democratic nomination for president, and Representative Elijah E. Cummings, Democrat of Maryland.

Doxycycline, an antibiotic, went from $20 a bottle in October 2013 to $1,849 by April 2014, according to the two lawmakers.

The Infectious Diseases Society of America and the HIV Medicine Association sent a joint letter to Turing earlier this month calling the price increase for Daraprim "unjustifiable for the medically vulnerable patient population" and "unsustainable for the health care system." An organization representing the directors of state AIDS programs has also been looking into the price increase, according to doctors and patient advocates.

Daraprim, known generically as pyrimethamine, is used mainly to treat toxoplasmosis, a parasite infection that can cause serious or even life-threatening problems for babies born to women who become infected during pregnancy, and also for people with compromised immune systems, like AIDS patients and certain cancer patients.

Martin Shkreli, the founder and chief executive of Turing, said that the drug is so rarely used that the impact on the health system would be minuscule and that Turing would use the money it earns to develop better treatments for toxoplasmosis, with fewer side effects.

"This isn't the greedy drug company trying to gouge patients, it is us trying to stay in business," Mr. Shkreli said. He said that many patients use the drug for far less than a year and that the price was now more in line with those of other drugs for rare diseases.

"This is still one of the smallest pharmaceutical products in the world," he said. "It really doesn't make sense to get any criticism for this."

RICHARD PERRY/THE NEW YORK TIMES

Martin Shkreli, chief executive and founder of Turing Pharmaceuticals, in his Manhattan office.

This is not the first time the 32-year-old Mr. Shkreli, who has a reputation for both brilliance and brashness, has been the center of controversy. He started MSMB Capital, a hedge fund company, in his 20s and drew attention for urging the Food and Drug Administration not to approve certain drugs made by companies whose stock he was shorting.

In 2011, Mr. Shkreli started Retrophin, which also acquired old neglected drugs and sharply raised their prices. Retrophin's board fired Mr. Shkreli a year ago. Last month, it filed a complaint in Federal District Court in Manhattan, accusing him of using Retrophin as a personal piggy bank to pay back angry investors in his hedge fund.

Mr. Shkreli has denied the accusations. He has filed for arbitration against his old company, which he says owes him at least $25 million in severance. "They are sort of concocting this wild and crazy and unlikely story to swindle me out of the money," he said.

Daraprim, which is also used to treat malaria, was approved by the F.D.A. in 1953 and has long been made by GlaxoSmithKline. Glaxo sold United States marketing rights to CorePharma in 2010. Last year, Impax Laboratories agreed to buy Core and affiliated companies for $700 million. In August, Impax sold Daraprim to Turing for $55 million, a deal announced the same day Turing said it had raised $90 million from Mr. Shkreli and other investors in its first round of financing.

Daraprim cost only about $1 a tablet several years ago, but the drug's price rose sharply after CorePharma acquired it. According to IMS Health, which tracks prescriptions, sales of the drug jumped to $6.3 million in 2011 from $667,000 in 2010, even as prescriptions held steady at about 12,700. In 2014, after further price increases, sales were $9.9 million, as the number of prescriptions shrank to 8,821. The figures do not include inpatient use in hospitals.

Turing's price increase could bring sales to tens or even hundreds of millions of dollars a year if use remains constant. Medicaid and certain hospitals will be able to get the drug inexpensively under federal rules for discounts and rebates. But private insurers, Medicare and hospitalized patients would have to pay an amount closer to the list price.

Some doctors questioned Turing's claim that there was a need for better drugs, saying the side effects, while potentially serious, could be managed.

"I certainly don't think this is one of those diseases where we have been clamoring for better therapies," said Dr. Wendy Armstrong, professor of infectious diseases at Emory University in Atlanta.

With the price now high, other companies could conceivably make generic copies, since patents have long expired. One factor that could discourage that option is that Daraprim's distribution is now tightly controlled, making it harder for generic companies to get the samples they need for the required testing.

The switch from drugstores to controlled distribution was made in June by Impax, not by Turing. Still, controlled distribution was a strategy Mr. Shkreli talked about at his previous company as a way to thwart generics.

Some hospitals say they now have trouble getting the drug. "We've not had access to the drug for a few months," said Dr. Armstrong, who also works at Grady Memorial Hospital, a huge public treatment center in Atlanta that serves many low-income patients.

But Dr. Rima McLeod, medical director of the toxoplasmosis center at the University of Chicago, said that Turing had been good about delivering drugs quickly to patients, sometimes without charge.

"They have jumped every time I've called," she said. The situation, she added, "seems workable" despite the price increase.

Daraprim is the standard first treatment for toxoplasmosis, in combination with an antibiotic called sulfadiazine. There are alternative treatments, but there is less data supporting their efficacy.

Dr. Aberg of Mount Sinai said some hospitals will now find Daraprim too expensive to keep in stock, possibly resulting in treatment delays. She said that Mount Sinai was continuing to use the drug, but each use now required a special review.

"This seems to be all profit-driven for somebody," Dr. Aberg said, "and I just think it's a very dangerous process."

Big Price Increase for Tuberculosis Drug Is Rescinded

BY ANDREW POLLACK | SEPT. 21, 2015

A HUGE OVERNIGHT price increase for an important tuberculosis drug has been rescinded after the company that acquired the drug gave it back to its previous owner under pressure, it was announced on Monday.

However, outrage over a gigantic price increase for another drug spread into the political sphere on Monday, causing biotechnology stocks to fall broadly as investors worried about possible government action to control pharmaceutical prices. The Nasdaq Biotechnology Index fell more than 4 percent.

"Price-gouging like this in the specialty drug market is outrageous," Hillary Rodham Clinton, a contender for the Democratic presidential nomination, said in a tweet on Monday. She said she would announce a plan on Tuesday to deal with rising drug prices.

Ms. Clinton was referring to the actions of Turing Pharmaceuticals, which last month acquired Daraprim, a 62-year-old drug used to treat a serious parasitic infection, and raised its price to $750 per tablet, from $13.50.

The cases of Daraprim and of the tuberculosis drug, cycloserine, are examples of a relatively new business strategy — acquiring old, neglected drugs, often for rare diseases, and turning them into costly "specialty" drugs.

Cycloserine was acquired last month by Rodelis Therapeutics, which promptly raised the price to $10,800 for 30 capsules, from $500. But the company agreed to return the drug to its former owner, a nonprofit organization affiliated with Purdue University, the organization said on Monday.

"We discovered literally on Thursday the strategy that had been undertaken" by Rodelis, said Dan Hasler, the president of the Purdue

Research Foundation, which has oversight of the manufacturing operation. "We said this was not what we had intended."

By Saturday, he said, Rodelis had agreed to give back the drug. Rodelis confirmed this in a brief statement on its website.

The foundation now will charge $1,050 for 30 capsules, twice what it charged before, but far less than Rodelis was charging. Mr. Hasler said the new price was needed to stem losses.

Cycloserine is used to treat multidrug-resistant tuberculosis, a serious form of the disease that does not respond to the usual drugs. There are only about 90 new cases a year in the United States, Mr. Hasler said, and about half those patients get treated with cycloserine.

Turing does not appear ready to surrender. Turing's founder and chief executive, Martin Shkreli, a former hedge fund manager, used television interviews and also Twitter and Reddit to defend his move.

He said that toxoplasmosis, the infection Daraprim is used to treat, had been ignored by the pharmaceutical industry because there was little money to be made. Now that Turing can presumably make money, he said, it will be able to educate doctors about the disease, improve delivery to patients and develop better drugs for the infection.

Infectious disease specialists, who have protested the price increase, question the need for new drugs for toxoplasmosis and say that if Turing wants to develop such drugs, it should use money from investors. They say the price increase will raise the cost of treating some adult patients with toxoplasmosis to hundreds of thousands of dollars a year.

Senator Bernie Sanders of Vermont, who is also vying for the Democratic presidential nomination, sent Turing a letter on Monday demanding information on the price increase.

"Without fast access to this drug, used to treat a very serious parasitic infection, patients may experience organ failure, blindness or death," Mr. Sanders said in a statement issued with Representative Elijah Cummings, Democrat of Maryland. The two lawmakers have been investigating sharp price increases in drugs, many of them old generics.

Rodelis, which increased the price of the tuberculosis drug, said last week it needed to invest to make sure the supply of the drug remained reliable. Rodelis reveals almost no information about itself, such as the names of its executives, directors or investors, on its web page.

Cycloserine, which went on sale in 1955 and is also known by the brand name Seromycin, was long produced by Eli Lilly and Company, which around 2000 decided to drop the drug, in part because the company was getting out of antibiotics.

Starting in 2003, as part of a philanthropic initiative on TB, Lilly transferred rights and manufacturing skill to generic drug companies in India, China, South Africa and elsewhere to supply the regions most affected. In 2007 it gave the rights for the United States and Canada to the Chao Center for Industrial Pharmacy and Contract Manufacturing, which is under the auspices of the Purdue Research Foundation.

Mr. Hasler, a former Lilly executive, said the Chao Center had lost about $10 million on the drug since 2007 because of the small number of patients and high regulatory costs. So the Chao Center was interested when it was approached by Rodelis. "They found us," Mr. Hasler said.

A patient with multidrug-resistant tuberculosis might take two capsules a day of cycloserine, along with other drugs, for 18 to 24 months, according to the Centers for Disease Control and Prevention. Under the price Rodelis planned to charge, a full course of treatment would have cost more than $500,000 for cycloserine alone. With the new price from the Chao Center, it will be closer to $50,000.

The drug made by generic companies abroad costs only about $20 for 100 capsules.

Amir Attaran, an expert on pharmaceutical access issues at the University of Ottawa, said it would have made much more sense to just import the drug from abroad, rather than have it produced in America for so few patients at such high cost.

Mr. Hasler said this was probably not done because foreign manufacturers were not willing to bear the expense of applying for regulatory approval in the United States.

Dr. Attaran said Lilly should have kept more control over pricing. "There's an obligation on their part, having transferred this, to ensure that the objective of the philanthropic initiative continues to be met," he said.

Lilly said that to comply with antitrust rules it retained no control over pricing once it transferred the rights to the Chao Center and had no say when Chao transferred the rights to Rodelis.

Valeant Under Investigation for Its Drug Pricing Practices

BY ANDREW POLLACK | OCT. 14, 2015

VALEANT PHARMACEUTICALS International, which has come under fire for aggressively increasing the prices of its drugs, said late Wednesday that it had received two federal subpoenas related to its pricing, distribution and patient support practices.

The subpoenas were issued by the United States attorney's offices in Manhattan and Massachusetts.

The company said that most of the material requested concerned the company's patient assistance programs. They also included requests related to distribution of the company's products, information provided to the Centers for Medicare & Medicaid Services, and the company's pricing decisions.

Patient assistance programs, such as when a company covers a patient's co-payment, can help patients get a drug they might not otherwise be able to afford. But that means that Medicaid, Medicare or commercial insurers have to pay for the drug.

It is not unusual for drug companies to receive subpoenas, and in some cases investigations do not result in any charges or settlements.

Valeant's stock has been weak in the last month as attention has become focused on companies that have sharply raised prices of old drugs. Valeant attracted scrutiny from some members of Congress for acquiring two old heart drugs, Isuprel and Nitropress, in February and immediately increasing their prices by more than 500 percent and 200 percent.

Last month, Senator Claire McCaskill, a Missouri Democrat, criticized the company for failing to respond substantively to a request for information she had made in August. In its announcement on Wednesday, Valeant said it had provided information on pricing to Senator McCaskill.

Valeant also said that it was beginning to reach out to hospitals affected by the price increases.

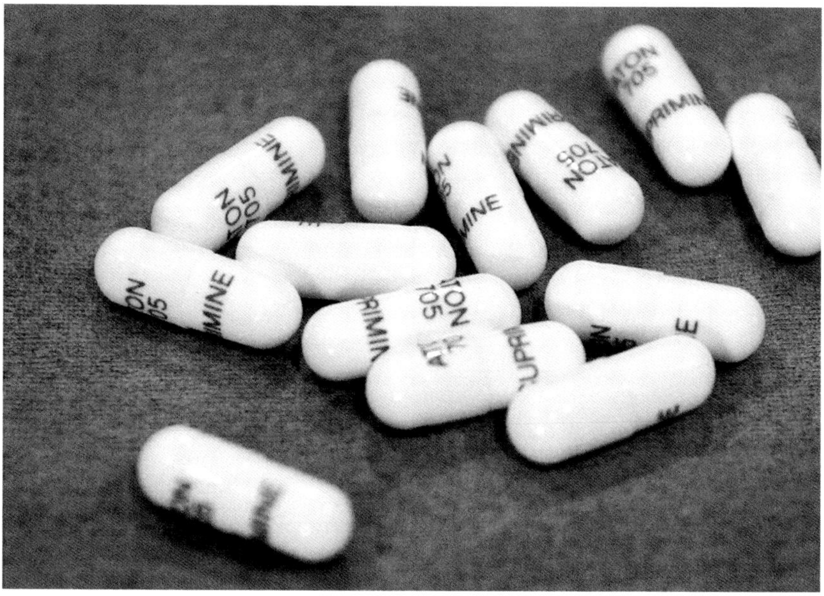

EMILY ROSE BENNETT FOR THE NEW YORK TIMES

Cuprimine, a drug used to treat Wilson disease.

Valeant said it would cooperate with the inquiries.

"All of us at Valeant firmly believe in maintaining strong regulatory and financial controls and believe we have operated our business in a fully compliant manner," J. Michael Pearson, the company's chief executive, said in a statement. He said the company remained "committed to assisting eligible patients who need our products."

Valeant has raised prices on many of its drugs, drawing the wrath of patients as well as hospitals. Some Wall Street reports show that Valeant is far more aggressive in raising prices than its peers.

VALEANT'S HISTORY OF DEAL MAKING

The drug company is known for growing through acquisitions and cutting costs.

A report issued on Wednesday by Sector & Sovereign Research, a stock research firm, said that Valeant's reliance on raising the prices of the drugs it sells in the United States was "extreme."

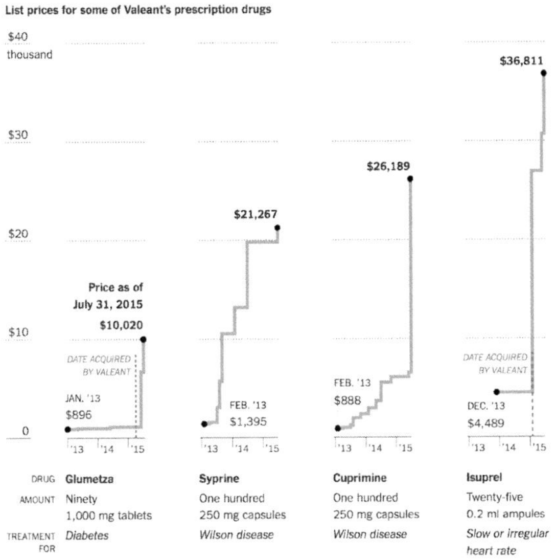

THE NEW YORK TIMES

Valeant Pharmaceuticals has made a business of buying prescription drugs and raising their prices when possible. Now some members of Congress are demanding information from the company about price increases on two heart drugs, one of which is Isuprel.

It said the average price of the company's prescription drugs had grown 48 percent a year since 2007. The volume of drugs it sold declined by 18 percent a year, resulting in a net gain in United States prescription drug sales of 32 percent a year.

In the past year, the report said, the situation was "even more dramatic," with pricing gains of 93 percent offsetting volume declines of 39 percent to yield net sales growth of 55 percent.

Some of the furor over drug prices was incited by Turing Pharmaceuticals, which acquired a 62-year-old drug for an infection and raised the price fiftyfold overnight.

The New York State attorney general's office has started an inquiry into Turing's distribution practices. On Wednesday, the Twitter account of Martin Shkreli, Turing's outspoken founder and chief executive, was suspended for reasons that are unclear.

Senators Condemn Big Price Increases for Drugs

BY ANDREW POLLACK | DEC. 9, 2015

SENATORS FROM BOTH parties on Wednesday denounced huge overnight price increases for decades-old drugs that have been made by some pharmaceutical companies lately, calling them unconscionable and detrimental to patients.

"These companies are to ethical pharmaceutical companies as a loan shark is to a bank," said Senator Susan Collins, Republican of Maine, quoting an unnamed industry specialist with whom she had spoken. She discussed the matter at a hearing of the Senate's Special Committee on Aging, which she leads.

The hearing focused on two companies in particular, Turing Pharmaceuticals, which acquired an old drug for a parasitic infection and raised the price to $750 a pill from $13.50, and Valeant Pharmaceuticals International, which has sharply increased the prices of various drugs it has acquired, including two used by hospitals to treat serious heart conditions.

The chief executives of these companies were not at the hearing, but that did not stop them from being criticized. Senator Claire McCaskill of Missouri, the ranking Democrat on the committee, mocked Martin Shkreli, the chief executive of Turing, by calling him "Mr. Wu-Tang." That was a reference to the news that Mr. Shkreli, 32, a former hedge fund manager, was revealed as the mystery buyer of the only known copy of a new album by Wu-Tang Clan.

Most of the hearing, which was described as the first in a series, was devoted to looking at the impact of the sudden price increases on doctors, patients and hospitals.

Erin R. Fox, director of the drug information service at University of Utah Health Care, said that the price of Isuprel, a heart drug acquired by Valeant early this year, was now $2,700 a vial compared with $440 before the acquisition and $50 two years ago. The hospital system would have had to spend $1.6 million extra a year just on that drug, she said, unless it curtailed it use.

So Isuprel was removed from the crash carts that are used in emergencies, Ms. Fox said, though it is still available from the pharmacy if doctors really need it. "Our physicians are incredibly frustrated" that they have to think twice about using the drug, she said.

Dr. David Kimberlin, a pediatric infectious disease specialist at the University of Alabama at Birmingham, recounted a case in which a baby needed Daraprim, the drug acquired by Turing, which increased its price to $750 a pill. Daraprim, acquired in August, treats toxoplasmosis, a parasitic infection that can cause blindness and brain damage.

Since Daraprim is a pill, it had to be turned into a liquid form that a baby could swallow. But the compounding pharmacy the hospital relied on to do that could not obtain the drug because of new restrictions Turing had placed on distribution. The huge price increase, which would bring the cost of a yearlong course of treatment for a baby to more than $69,000 from $1,200, was also a deterrent.

"Babies' lives literally hang in the balance here," Dr. Kimberlin said. He said that infectious disease societies had surveyed members and found more than 30 cases in which people had trouble obtaining Daraprim promptly.

In a statement, Turing said it was committed to developing innovative therapies and was making sure that no patient was denied access to Daraprim. Valeant said in a statement that "broad conclusions about the company's pricing cannot be drawn from any one drug" and that most hospitals use small amounts of Isuprel, limiting any impact of price increases.

Ms. Fox and others who testified said that companies like Turing and Valeant were able to increase prices so rapidly because of a lack of competition in the market for generic drugs, which stemmed in part from consolidation in that industry. The lack of competition plus manufacturing problems have led to shortages and price increases for antibiotics, anesthetics and some other drugs that are more widely used than Daraprim and Isuprel.

Various suggestions were made for dealing with the issue. Gerard Anderson, a professor at the Johns Hopkins Bloomberg School of Public Health, said the Food and Drug Administration should expedite approval of generic drugs for economic reasons.

Daraprim and Isuprel have no patent protection but there are no generic competitors either, because the market was small until the big price hikes. If a generic company wanted to enter now, it could take two to three years to get F.D.A. approval. But if that time could be reduced to six months, it would provide a deterrent to huge price hikes, he said.

Express Scripts, the largest pharmacy benefit manager, is encouraging use of an alternative to Daraprim that is made by a compounding pharmacy and sells for about $1 a pill. But witnesses at the hearing were reluctant to recommend more use of compounding to save money because such drugs are not approved by the F.D.A. and have had safety issues in the past.

"Compounding should not be a blanket, one-size-fits-all solution," said Ms. Fox of the University of Utah.

Mark Merritt, chief of the Pharmaceutical Care Management Association, which represents pharmacy benefit managers, called for a watch list of drugs with no generic competition that would be vulnerable to huge price increases. He said there were about 200 such drugs.

"The hedge funds have these lists, the government may as well too," he said.

No Justification for High Drug Prices

EDITORIAL | BY THE NEW YORK TIMES | DEC. 19, 2015

THERE IS AMPLE evidence that drug prices have been pushed to astronomical heights for no reason other than the desire of drug makers to maximize profits. Prices in many cases far exceed what's needed to cover the costs of research and clinical trials, and some companies have found ways to rake in profits even without shouldering the cost of drug development.

The two worst offenders are bottom feeders that simply buy companies they believe have underpriced their drugs and then quickly raise prices to astronomical levels.

In August, Turing Pharmaceuticals acquired the American marketing rights to a 62-year-old drug to treat a devastating parasitic infection and raised the cost of one pill to $750 from $13.50. That brought the cost of a course of treatment for some patients to hundreds of thousands of dollars. (Turing's founder, Martin Shkreli, was indicted on Thursday on charges of securities fraud involving a hedge fund and another biotechnology firm he started.)

Valeant Pharmaceuticals greatly increased the prices of several drugs it acquired, including two used by hospitals to treat heart conditions. It also protected its high-priced dermatology drugs by urging doctors to send prescriptions to a mail-order pharmacy that would make sure no cheaper alternative was substituted.

The Pharmaceutical Research and Manufacturers of America, a trade group, described Turing and Valeant as essentially investment vehicles "masquerading as pharmaceutical companies."

Yet even some mainstream companies have set high prices that seem hard to justify. Eli Lilly said its new lung cancer drug, Portrazza, would cost about $11,430 a month in the United States, six times the $1,870 price that leading oncologists said in a recent journal article would be a fair reflection of the benefit the drug offers compared with older therapies.

Similarly, Pfizer set the list price for Ibrance, a drug to treat a form of advanced breast cancer, at $9,850 a month, a price that remains high even after the 20 percent discount demanded by insurers. The price was not based on manufacturing costs or research costs, according to an analysis by The Wall Street Journal. Rather, Pfizer set the price as high as it could without causing doctors and insurers to favor an alternative drug.

The pharmaceutical industry often defends its prices by noting that drugs account for only 10 percent of nationwide health spending. But in employer-based health insurance plans, drug benefits account for 19 percent of spending, not much less than spending on inpatient hospital care, according to a recent analysis by the Kaiser Family Foundation. And surveys have shown that many Americans have difficulty paying for the drugs they need. Major drug companies often increase prices 10 percent or more a year, far faster than inflation, straining the health care system.

Experts have proposed several ways to reduce drug prices, like fostering greater competition among drug companies or allowing the government to negotiate lower prices. Encouraging the development of innovative drugs and setting prices in ways that make lifesaving medicines affordable to all are not mutually exclusive ideas.

Another Drug Pricing Ripoff

EDITORIAL | BY THE NEW YORK TIMES | AUG. 25, 2016

THE RAPID INCREASE in the price of the EpiPen, a device used to give an injection that can save people from deadly allergic reactions, has shocked consumers and lawmakers. Yet it is just one more outrageous instance of pharmaceutical companies raising prices for lifesaving medicines with no justification other than the desire to increase profits — and doing so knowing that government can do little about it.

EpiPens have been used since 1977 to deliver epinephrine to people suffering anaphylaxis, an allergic reaction that causes the body to go into shock and air passages to narrow. If not treated quickly, the condition can lead to death. People allergic to peanuts, bee stings and other things often carry these auto-injections with them at all times.

Mylan, which sells the EpiPen, has raised the wholesale price from less than $100 for a two-pack in 2007 when it acquired the product from Merck KGaA, to about $600 in May. Those price increases and more marketing helped boost sales to about $1 billion, from $200 million, Bloomberg News reported last year.

Some consumers say they can no longer afford EpiPens and are relying on old EpiPens, which may not be as effective because the devices expire after a year. Emergency medical services in some cities are now using syringes and epinephrine vials, which cost much less but can be harder to use. A competing product, Adrenaclick, also costs less but some insurers do not cover it and many doctors do not prescribe it because it is not as well known.

Several members of Congress are calling on Mylan to explain its price increases. Experts say that the device has not changed much in recent years, which would rule out the need to recoup research and development costs, a common industry explanation for high prices.

Senator Amy Klobuchar, Democrat of Minnesota, has asked the Federal Trade Commission to investigate whether Mylan has used illegal tactics to dominate this market by, for example, getting insurers not to cover and pharmacies not to stock competing products. She has also asked for Senate hearings.

High-level scrutiny from Ms. Klobuchar and others could conceivably shame Mylan into lowering prices. But if Congress were concerned about escalating drug prices, it would undertake a much broader look at the industry and possible legislative remedies. Mylan is hardly alone. Prescription drug prices jumped 38 percent in the last 10 years, compared to an 18 percent increase in general inflation, according to the Bureau of Labor Statistics.

One reason for those increases is that Congress doesn't let Medicare negotiate prescription drug prices. Many medicines cost significantly less in other developed countries, like Canada and Britain, which do negotiate with drug makers. Pharmaceutical companies have also squelched competition by, in effect, paying one another to delay the introduction of generic drugs. The Supreme Court ruled in 2013 that regulators could challenge such agreements on antitrust grounds, but did not declare those deals illegal. Congress should pass legislation that would make pay-for-delay agreements illegal.

But many in Congress are ideologically opposed to giving the government more control or are unwilling to vote against the interests of the drug industry, which donates generously to political campaigns. Until that changes, the cost of medicines will continue to escalate.

The EpiPen, a Case Study in Health System Dysfunction

BY AARON E. CARROLL | AUG. 23, 2016

THREE TIMES IN the last two weeks, people — a patient, a colleague and my wife — told me stories about how out of control the price of EpiPens were. Monday, my New York Times colleagues recounted in detail how expensive the devices have become in recent years. All tell the tale of how much even basic health care can cost in the United States.

But by digging a bit further, the story of EpiPens can also explain so much of what's wrong with our health care system.

When people think of allergies to drugs, food or a bee sting, they often think of a rash. And in fact that's how many allergic reactions develop and proceed. Most can be treated with diphenhydramine (Benadryl) and careful observation. But some are more serious. Between 1 and 2 percent of people can develop what's known as anaphylaxis, when the airways you need to breathe swell and close.

Luckily, there's a simple treatment for such reactions. Epinephrine — or adrenaline — is a hormone naturally produced by the adrenal glands. It's part of your "fight or flight" response, and it causes your heart to beat faster, your blood vessels to constrict, your pupils to dilate and — most important here — your airways to open.

Epinephrine is very, very cheap. Even in the developing world, it costs less than a dollar per milliliter, and there's less than a third of that in an EpiPen.

But to save a life, epinephrine must be delivered quickly, and in the proper amounts. People suffering severe allergic reactions often can't do it themselves. Drawing the drug into a syringe and then administering it to someone else requires training and precision that most people lack.

For that, there is the EpiPen.

What makes this auto-injection device so special is not the drug, but the ease with which it automatically administers the correct dose without delay. The instructions are right on the side, and even if you don't read them, it's pretty easy to figure out. Pull off the safety cap, put the tip against the thigh, and push. Boom. Epinephrine delivered.

The EpiPen isn't new; it has been in use since 1977. Research and development costs were recouped long ago. Nine years ago, it was bought by the pharmaceutical company Mylan, which then began to sell the device. When Mylan bought it, EpiPens cost about $57 each.

Few competitors existed, and for various reasons, that has remained the case. The device actually worked and saved lives. People needed it. Mylan raised the price. It also began to raise awareness.

Unfortunately, epinephrine is inherently unstable. Research shows that it degrades pretty quickly over time, and it's recommended that EpiPens be replaced every year. When my friends ask me if they can take an expired over-the-counter pain medication like acetaminophen or ibuprofen, I shrug and nod. If they don't get a full dose, it's usually not a big deal. But epinephrine is no joke. People in anaphylaxis need a full dose every time. They therefore need to replace all their EpiPens every year, again and again.

Kids need them in many places. They need them at home. They need them at school. They need them at camp. They may even want to stash one at Grandma's house. So people often need to buy quite a few.

More revenue for Mylan. And it raised the price.

Then in 2010, federal guidelines changed to recommend that two EpiPens be sold in a package instead of one. Studies showed that about 10 percent of children who received epinephrine from an EpiPen needed more than one dose. Better to be safe than sorry. Additionally, the Food and Drug Administration changed its recommendations to allow for the prescription of EpiPens for prevention for at-risk patients, not just for those with confirmed allergies. Mylan stopped selling individual EpiPens and began to sell only twin-packs.

It also raised the price.

In 2013, the government went further. It passed a law that gave funding preferences for asthma treatment grants to states that maintained an emergency supply of EpiPens. As the near sole supplier of the devices, Mylan stood to make even more money.

That year, Mylan raised the price again.

Of course, competition would bring the price down. But it's very hard to bring such a device to market. In 2012, the Adrenaclick and Twinject were discontinued. In 2013, Sanofi began to sell Auvi-Q devices, which even gave audio instructions to walk people though their use. Unfortunately, they were found to give potentially improper doses, and were pulled from the shelves about a year ago.

Teva had hoped to offer a generic version of the EpiPen, but concerns from the F.D.A. sent it back to the drawing board until at least next year.

Adamis hoped to offer prefilled syringes, which would still be harder to use than EpiPens. But it was told by the F.D.A. that much more data would be needed before such a product could be sold.

These setbacks, all in the last year, have once again left Mylan with a veritable run of the market. It raised the price of EpiPens again. As of this May, they cost more than $600 a pack. Since 2004, after adjusting for inflation, the price of EpiPens has risen more than 450 percent.

An alternative still exists. The Adrenaclick, while still not cheap, is back and less expensive than the EpiPen. Some think it's harder to use, though. It's not on the accepted list for many health insurance plans. More important, few physicians think of it. Because of that, they write prescriptions for EpiPens. Since the Adrenaclick is not a generic version of the EpiPen, pharmacists can't substitute one for the other. A prescription for an EpiPen must be filled with an EpiPen, regardless of what consumers might want.

Some people argue that we could still just use syringes and epinephrine for far less money. Sure, they would expire every few months. Sure, they would be harder to use and likelier to break. Sure, they would require training, be hard for the uninitiated to use in an emergency and be more likely to be administered with an incorrect dose. Nonetheless, you could argue that they're an alternative when the "Cadillac" EpiPens are financially out of reach.

But those are unsatisfactory arguments. Epinephrine isn't an elective medication. It doesn't last, so people need to purchase the drug repeatedly. There's little competition, but there are huge hurdles to enter the market, so a company can raise the price again and again with little pushback. The government encourages the product's use, but makes no effort to control its cost. Insurance coverage shields some from the expense, allowing higher prices, but leaves those most at-risk most exposed to extreme out-of-pocket outlays. The poor are the most likely to consider going without because they can't afford it.

EpiPens are a perfect example of a health care nightmare. They're also just a typical example of the dysfunction of the American health care system.

AARON E. CARROLL is a professor of pediatrics at Indiana University School of Medicine who blogs on health research and policy at The Incidental Economist and makes videos at Healthcare Triage.

The Complex Math Behind Spiraling Prescription Drug Prices

BY KATIE THOMAS | AUG. 24, 2016

THE SOARING COST of prescription drugs has generated outrage among politicians and patients. Some cancer drugs carry price tags of more than $100,000 a year, and health plans are increasingly asking people to shoulder a greater share of the cost.

The latest outrage involves the price of EpiPen, a lifesaving injection device for people with severe allergies, which has risen to more than $600 for the list price of a two-pen set, from less than $100 when Mylan acquired the product in 2007.

A bipartisan group of senators has demanded that Mylan explain why the cost of EpiPen has skyrocketed, and others have called for congressional hearings, like those that examined price increases by Turing Pharmaceuticals and Valeant Pharmaceuticals International.

In surveys, Americans routinely say drug prices are a top health care concern, and it has been an issue on the presidential campaign trail.

But there are no simple answers.

WHAT IS THE CONTROVERSY OVER DRUG PRICING ALL ABOUT?

Much of the attention has focused on a handful of pharmaceutical companies that have snapped up old drugs and then aggressively raised prices, sometimes by more than 1,000 percent. Last fall, Martin Shkreli, the founder and former chief executive of Turing Pharmaceuticals, ignited a fierce response on social media after it was reported that his company had raised the price of a little-known drug to treat toxoplasmosis to $750 a tablet from $13.50. And Valeant Pharmaceuticals International has received similar attention for raising the price of many of its drugs, including two heart medications, Nitropress and Isuprel.

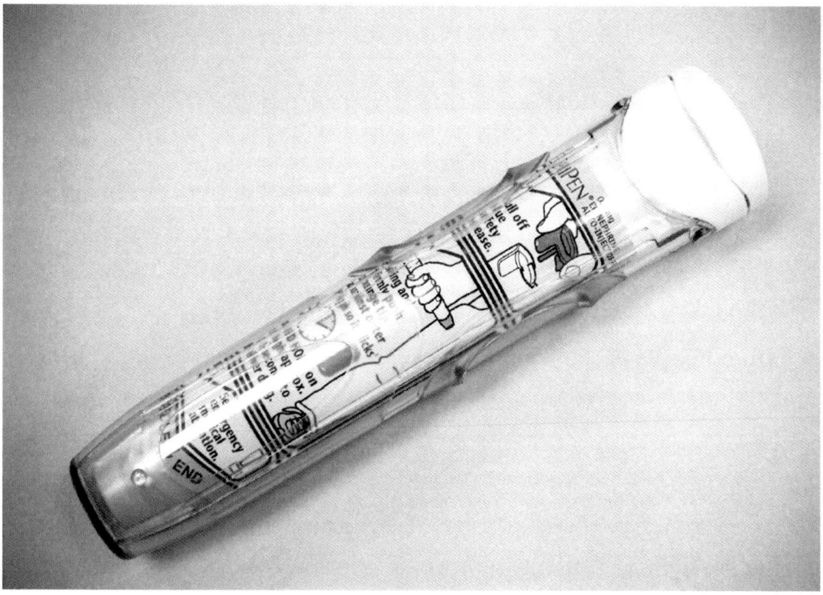

KAREN KASMAUSKI FOR THE NEW YORK TIMES

The EpiPen dispenses epinephrine, a drug that reverses symptoms of a severe reaction to allergens like peanuts.

Critics say these companies and others like them have unfairly favored profit over patients' needs. Congress has held several hearings on these tactics, and Valeant and Turing are under investigation by federal authorities. Presidential candidates have singled out these companies on the campaign trail.

But even as the drug industry has sought to distance itself from companies it describes as bad actors, insurers, hospitals and other major health care players have raised alarms about the rising cost of new drugs, including those that treat cancer, hepatitis C and rare diseases. Some of those drugs can cost $300,000 a year.

Higher drug prices threaten to raise insurance premiums and patients' out-of-pocket expenses and can cost taxpayers more because of Medicaid and other government programs. But drug companies say the prices reflect the enormous investment of time and resources that go into bringing a drug to market and argue that many times, their drugs can prevent more expensive medical interventions like surgery and hospitalization.

SO HOW MUCH DO DRUGS COST?

The answer to this is more complicated than one might expect.

Manufacturers set list prices for their brand-name drugs; those are the eye-popping figures that have sent Congress and presidential candidates into fits of outrage.

But almost no one actually pays those prices. Insurers and pharmacy-benefit managers, who manage drug plans for insurers, negotiate discounts and rebates, which lowers the effective cost of a drug. And they have been getting better at doing this.

That is why, although list prices for drugs rose about 12 percent in 2015, net prices — what insurers and employers actually paid — grew only about 2.8 percent, the lowest rate in years, according to IMS Health, a research firm.

Insurers and others say that lower figure obscures the larger price increases in specific areas like cancer treatment, where less competition exists and it is more difficult to pit manufacturers against one another. In the case of EpiPen, Mylan has a virtual monopoly after a similar product was withdrawn from the market about a year ago.

What's more, drug makers do profit from raising their list prices because rebates and discounts are often based on a percentage of those prices.

"That's where the real angst in the marketplace is," said Steve Miller, chief medical officer of Express Scripts.

WHO TAKES A PIECE OF A DRUG'S PRICE?

A drug's path from the manufacturer to the patient is circuitous, and many middlemen are paid along the way.

The pharmaceutical company sends the drug to a distributor, which takes a fee and then sells the drug to a pharmacy, which pockets its own fee before dispensing the medication to a patient. If a patient is insured, a pharmacy-benefit manager is paid for processing the transaction between the pharmacy and the insurer or employer. The pharmacy-benefit manager also handles the rebates that flow from the drug maker to the insurer or the employer.

Part of what makes the issue so frustrating is that visiting a pharmacy to pick up a prescription seems simple. "If you go into a retail pharmacy, it looks like a retail transaction," said Adam J. Fein, president of Pembroke Consulting, a management advisory and business research company. But it is not like buying a bottle of orange juice; most patients do not choose which drug they are picking up, nor are they paying for most of it, he said. "It's part of this crazy system."

WHAT DOES THIS MEAN FOR PATIENTS?

The good news first: The vast majority of drugs dispensed in the United States — more than 80 percent — are generics, which are low-cost alternatives to brand-name drugs. If your doctor writes you a prescription, there is a very good chance it will cost you $10 or less.

But if you have a more serious illness or require a newer, brand-name drug, insurers have been requiring that you pay an increasingly large share of the drug's cost.

Many people are covered by health plans with large deductibles that require them to pay the full price of their drugs until they hit their limit, which can be thousands of dollars a year. And more plans are requiring patients who need expensive specialty drugs to contribute a percentage of the list price. Drug companies often help cover patients' out-of-pocket costs through assistance programs, but not always.

So patients who are the sickest and require the most expensive drugs are the most vulnerable to soaring drug prices.

"It's sort of embedded in the health care system that the price is never the price, unless you're a cash-paying customer," Mr. Fein said. "And in that case, we soak the poor."

The Lesson of EpiPens: Why Drug Prices Spike, Again and Again

OPINION | BY ELISABETH ROSENTHAL | SEPT. 2, 2016

WHEN I WAS a kid in the late 1960s, I suffered from serious asthma attacks. About twice each summer, struggling for air, I received a shot of epinephrine drawn up in a syringe from the camp nurse. The relief was nothing short of miraculous.

Today that same tiny, lifesaving bolus of epinephrine — used mostly to treat severe allergic reactions — is delivered via sometimes elaborate devices called auto-injectors. Though the medicine itself hasn't changed, the delivery devices have been protected by patents, enabling drug makers to charge ever escalating — sometimes prohibitive — prices for one of the oldest drugs in medical use.

Though Mylan, the maker of the EpiPen auto-injector, had been raising prices by 20 percent annually in recent years without much blowback, it set off political outrage last month by raising the price to over $600 for two pens just before parents were buying new EpiPens for their school-bound children. Heather Bresch, the chief executive of Mylan, suddenly found herself in the same penalty box as Martin Shkreli, the pharma bad boy, who last year raised the price of an old drug for parasites, Daraprim, by over 5,000 percent. Members of Congress called for hearings. Hillary Clinton denounced Mylan on Twitter.

To mitigate the widespread outrage, Mylan first announced that it would give insured patients $300 coupons to offset the higher price and then, last week, that it would make a cheaper generic version of its own product. Patients may have, once again, won a battle. But they are losing the war on high drug prices.

Ms. Bresch was in many ways acting in accordance with a core strategy in the pharmaceutical industry's playbook — take something old and repackage it to make it new and patentable — and then see what price the market will bear. Sometimes extortionate prices are

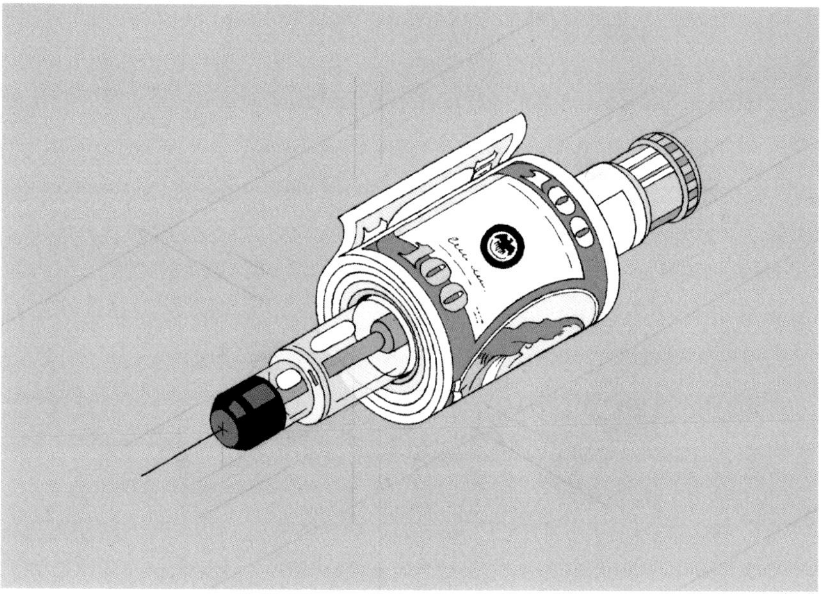

STEFAN GLERUM

a predictable outcome. Yet the government has no real tools to curb them.

Many other old medications have been delivered in new packages in recent years, with startling price increases. Basic asthma inhalers, which once cost under $15 (and still do in many countries), cost $50 to $100 in the United States. A portion of the big price rises for insulin in recent years is attributable to new types of injectors to deliver the medicine. Long-off-patent emergency rescue drugs delivered by auto-injector — not just epinephrine, but also naloxone to reverse opiate overdose — have seen particularly perplexing price escalations.

New devices can make it more convenient and safer to deliver a lifesaving drug during a medical crisis. But when is new packaging — often accompanied by bells and whistles of uncertain value — worth an exponential rise in price? That's something a nation struggling with a $3 trillion health bill must consider, and it merits a response beyond a few days of executive public shaming.

Like so much in our overpriced medical system, today's EpiPen debacle evolved from a laudable idea: Though shots of epinephrine have been used for over a century, the EpiPen — invented in the mid-1970s and approved by the Food and Drug Administration in 1987 — allowed a patient or a parent to easily administer the proper dose in an emergency. When an unlocked EpiPen is pressed against the thigh, a needle emerges to inject the medicine, even through clothes.

In recent decades it has become an increasingly attractive idea commercially as well: Research suggests that the incidence of allergies has been growing (a trend relentlessly publicized by Mylan). Also, "the social frenzy around allergies has spurred substantial demand," said Dr. Aaron Kesselheim, an associate professor at Harvard Medical School and an author of an influential recent article about combating high drug prices, noting that many families buy multiple kits, for school, home and car. Schools and camps bought in — it was easier (and legally prudent, perhaps) to have auto-injectors at the ready, rather than to draw epinephrine into a syringe.

A dose of epinephrine, also known as adrenaline, costs about $1. But paying for a smoother delivery system might have seemed eminently reasonable when EpiPens retailed for $50, as they did in 2004. The cost-benefit calculation has become increasingly less rational as prices escalated — especially since the vast majority of EpiPens are thrown away when they expire after about 12 months, requiring another purchase.

Mylan has cleverly exploited market opportunities since it acquired the rights to the EpiPen in 2007. At first, it moved somewhat tentatively, slowly raising the price to about $250 by 2013.

That year, a start-up called Kaleo won approval for a talking injector, called Auvi-Q. "Now hold in place for five seconds," the voice intoned before giving a countdown. Its price was about $400.

Perhaps as a response, in late 2013, Mylan began a series of more aggressive price increases for the EpiPen kit, so what was then about $250 is now $600, and includes two EpiPens and a training device.

Other companies tried to sell other injectors at a slightly lower price, but competing with Mylan was tough, since the EpiPen seemed synonymous with the drug. One injector, Adrenaclick, costs $450, and as low as about $140 with a coupon for a two-pen kit.

"Doctors say, 'My patients know how to use the EpiPen.' Parents say, 'They're my kids, I trust this brand,' " said Doug Hirsch, the chief executive of GoodRx, a website that helps consumers shop for cheaper drugs. "People don't think there's a choice."

That perception became nearly gospel in 2015, when Auvi-Q was withdrawn from the market because of concerns about unreliable dosing. Mylan could almost set the price wherever it wanted.

Mylan has tried to calm the waters by offering many patients $300 coupons to cover increased co-payments. But that is a Band-Aid — and a deceptive, high-priced one at that: While we consumers may be insulated from the charge at the pharmacy counter, our insurers are paying the increased rates, leading to premium rises next year. And our schools buy EpiPens with our tax dollars.

Mylan's intention to make a generic EpiPen, though it will help some patients, is likewise a calculated maneuver. If Mylan is prepared to offer a $300 generic injector, made in the same factories with the same components, why doesn't it just sell the EpiPen for the lower price? The answer is all business and no medicine: Mylan can hang onto the market for doctors and patients who demand the trusted brand name, while cornering an incipient generic market.

There are many better solutions to price spikes: For example, Dr. Kesselheim suggests, the government could regard extreme prices as it does drug shortages, allowing for emergency imports of cheaper products. The United States patent office and the F.D.A. could be stingier in handing out market exclusivity for patents on drugs and delivery devices that offer little or no benefit. A national body could set price ceilings for essential medicines (as occurs in other countries), or review rate increases levied on products that are unchanged.

But hearings and a few days of uncomfortable interviews for Ms. Bresch (who makes $18 million a year) will not solve the underlying problem. The next EpiPen crisis is no doubt in the making, with patients already suffering from inexplicable rising prices for a much-needed drug, until that trip line of outrage is once again crossed.

ELISABETH ROSENTHAL, a former New York Times correspondent, is the editor in chief of Kaiser Health News and the author of the forthcoming "An American Sickness: How Healthcare Became Big Business and How to Take It Back."

CHAPTER 3

Disease Branding and the Profusion of Diagnoses

All products need viable markets. Drug manufacturers prime these markets by selling the diseases as hard as they sell the drugs that treat them. Two trends helped create a favorable market for manufacturers. The first was major advances in medicine and the understanding of what causes, and what can prevent, disease. As a result, manufacturers were able to broaden the use of a single medication by getting it approved for multiple indications or through "off-label" uses. Secondly, disease diagnoses have increased. This chapter examines the impact these issues have had, particularly on the diagnosis and treatment of A.D.H.D.

Ritalin Wars

OPINION | BY JUDITH WARNER | NOV. 15, 2007

THE SINKING FEELING came over me as soon as I saw the Page One headline: "Bad Behavior Does Not Doom Pupils, Studies Say: New Look at Attention Deficit Disorders as a Delay, Not a Flaw."

Here we go again, I thought. Another round in the Ritalin wars.

I barely had to read beyond the first two paragraphs

> *Educators and psychologists have long feared that children entering school with behavior problems were doomed to fall behind in the upper grades. But two new studies suggest that those fears are exaggerated.*

One concluded that kindergartners who are identified as troubled do as well academically as their peers in elementary school. The other found that children with attention deficit disorders suffer primarily from a delay in brain development, not from a deficit or flaw.

to know what the reaction to the story would be.

A ground-breaking new National Institute of Mental Health brain imaging study showing that the brains of kids with Attention-Deficit Hyperactivity Disorder were delayed in development? Indications that some kids eventually outgrow their symptoms? A major education study by researchers at a number of prestigious universities finding that bad classroom behavior (read: ADHD, as most readers did) doesn't lead to later academic failure?

Ammunition for the let-kids-be-kids critique of attention deficit hyperactivity disorder. Vindication for all those who believe that ADHD isn't a "disorder" at all. Validation for all those freewheeling, high-spirited kids who can't shut up or sit still. And, of course, scientific confirmation for the view that to medicate kids with attentional or behavioral issues is unnecessary, potentially injurious and cruel.

"First, get the child off pills!" wrote "Hazel," one of the first posters to the site the Times set up to welcome reader comments.

"It is a shame to treat normal children with drugs because they are a bit slow in development and are being forced to do things above their maturity level," concurred "jayne."

"We are medicating children to conform to chronological age expectations when we should be allowing them to develop at their normal pace," said "Lee."

"The fact that so many kids grew out of their A.D.H.D proves that parents, and doctors have been turning a whole generation of American children into drug users, unnecessarily," said "Jo."

"So much anger unleashed here," added "ald."

I came away from reading the Times and from listening to NPR ("Good news" announced Diane Rehm. "The brains of children who suffer from ADHD develop slightly later but without any long-term impairment") wondering if everything I'd learned about ADHD in three solid years of book research was wrong.

After all, as I'd come to understand it, ADHD is a disorder that dogs most sufferers throughout their lives. Its durability is part of what qualifies it as a "disorder," distinct from, let's say, situational, stressed-out or anxious distractability, childish immaturity or plain old bad behavior.

Not only does ADHD tend to last, I've read, and heard, again and again, it's associated with all kinds of bad outcomes over time: increased rates of depression, anxiety and substance abuse, and low self-esteem, at the very least. It was hard to believe that the new "good news" could turn decades of research on its ear. It was troubling, too.

So, as the brain imaging study wended its way through the week's news cycle, I contacted some of the leading minds on the subject of ADHD, including psychiatrists Philip Shaw, the lead author of the NIMH study, and Judith Rapoport, a co-author. I asked these clinicians and researchers if my understanding of ADHD had now been proven all wrong.

Had ADHD finally been shown to be a rather trivial disorder, of a type with the waywardness of natural boyhood, better left untreated, best handled through maturation, unconditional love and chemical-free good living?

Rapoport, who has been Chief of the Child Psychiatry Branch at the NIMH since 1984, was momentarily struck dumb by the question.

Shaw said, "That's certainly not what I would take away from this study."

Greg J. Duncan, a professor in the School of Education and Social Policy at Northwestern University and the lead author of the school study, was somewhat mystified that his research — which attempted to understand the links between kindergarteners' math, reading, attention-paying and "socioemotional" skills and their later academic achievement — was being discussed in the same breath with ADHD at all. The study, he said, wasn't "about clinical levels of attention problems."

This was true. Duncan's research didn't measure the effect of ADHD on future achievement; in fact, it made no mention of ADHD at all. There was mention of "attention skills" and "attention problems" — which did correlate with lesser academic achievement — and there was talk of "externalizing" behavior ("anti-social behavior, losing your temper, getting in fights, being disruptive," as Duncan defined it for me).

But neither attention problems nor bad behavior are synonyms for the very specific, clinically significant, impairment-causing disorder that is ADHD. "The term disruptive behavior hardly equates to the clinical diagnosis of ADHD," Russell A. Barkley, author, most recently, of "ADHD in Adults: What the Science Says," and of "Taking Charge of ADHD: The Complete, Authoritative Guide for Parents" told me via email.

In the popular mind, though, it does.

In fact, we tend these days to think that bad behavior — and bad boy behavior in particular — has been made synonymous with ADHD ("We used to have a word for sufferers of ADHD. We called them boys," quips a psychoanalyst in Christopher Lane's new book, "Shyness: How Normal Behavior Became a Sickness"). Our thinking this, however, doesn't mean that it is so. No matter how many times, or how fervently, the cliché is repeated.

"It's a shame the whole thing is so politicized," said Edward Hallowell, whose 1994 book, "Driven to Distraction," co-authored with John J. Ratey, put attention deficit on the national map.

ADHD belief, Hallowell sighed, has become like "religion."

Years of research back up the basic assertions of the NIMH study: that there are biological differences in the brains of people with ADHD, and that some people see their symptoms disappear over time. (Fully two-thirds of ADHD sufferers don't get entirely better, though, Shaw stressed to me. Their symptoms live on into adulthood and are "greatly impairing.")

So why, this week, did the gloves come out, with the armies of all that is Good taking on the usual forces of Evil psychopharmacology? Why did my stomach drop so quickly to my knees, why was I so quick to think it possible that, after countless interviews and lectures and hours of reading, I'd simply fallen for a hoax manufactured by the drug companies and foisted upon the innocent?

Facts don't have much sway when you're in the grip of a religion. And the beliefs underlying the Ritalin wars (I am using "Ritalin" here as shorthand for the whole practice of diagnosing children and treating them with psychotropic drugs) have truly now become like a creed. They're only superficially about diagnosis and medication. For most people, they're more profoundly about a sense of menace bearing down upon the world of our children.

There's a sense that greater powers, profit-driven and amoral, are pulling the strings in our children's lives. There's a sense that those who should best protect us — our government and our doctors — are so corrupted that they can no longer do the job. There's a sense that childhood has, in many ways, been denatured, that youth has been stolen, that the range of human acceptability has been narrowed for our kids to a point that it has become soul-crushingly inhuman.

I share all these feelings. I think that most of us do. But where I differ (now) from those eager to pile onto the anti-ADHD bandwagon is that I'm not willing — anymore — to sacrifice real children and their parents on the altar of ideology.

JUDITH WARNER is the author of "Perfect Madness: Motherhood in the Age of Anxiety" and a contributing columnist.

Disease Branding

OPINION | BY BEN SCHOTT | OCT. 18, 2010

Hyping the profile of a medical condition in order to sell its treatment.

WRITING FOR CNN, Carl Elliott compared the modern marketing of certain medicines with Edward Bernays's idea, in the 1920s, of selling pianos by popularizing the idea that sophisticates had music rooms:

> *Just as Bernays sold pianos by selling the music room, pharmaceutical marketers now sell drugs by selling the diseases that they treat. The buzzword is "disease branding."*
>
> *To brand a disease is to shape its public perception in order to make it more palatable to potential patients. Panic disorder, reflux disease, erectile dysfunction, restless legs syndrome, bipolar disorder, overactive bladder, ADHD, premenstrual dysphoric disorder, even clinical depression: All these conditions were once regarded as rare until a marketing campaign transformed the brand.*
>
> *Once a branded disease has achieved a degree of cultural legitimacy, there is no need to convince anyone that a drug to treat it is necessary. It will come to him as his own idea.*

According to Elliott, "disease branding" works best when a condition can be de-stigmatized, or when one can imply that a condition is under-diagnosed.

BEN SCHOTT is the author of "Schott's Original Miscellany," its two sequels, and the yearbook "Schott's Almanac." He is a contributing columnist to The New York Times's Op-Ed page.

It's Still the 'Age of Anxiety.' Or Is It?

OPINION | BY DANIEL SMITH | JAN. 14, 2012

IT'S HARD TO BELIEVE that anyone but scholars of modern literature or paid critics have read W.H. Auden's dramatic poem "The Age of Anxiety" all the way through, even though it won a Pulitzer Prize in 1948, the year after it was published. It is a difficult work — allusive, allegorical, at times surreal. But more to the point, it's boring. The characters meet, drink, talk and walk around; then they drink, talk and walk around some more. They do this for 138 pages; then they go home.

Auden's title, though: that people know. From the moment it appeared, the phrase has been used to characterize the consciousness of our era, the awareness of everything perilous about the modern world: the degradation of the environment, nuclear energy, religious fundamentalism, threats to privacy and the family, drugs, pornography, violence, terrorism. Since 1990, it has appeared in the title or subtitle of at least two dozen books on subjects ranging from science to politics to parenting to sex ("Mindblowing Sex in the Real World: Hot Tips for Doing It in the Age of Anxiety"). As a sticker on the bumper of the Western world, "the age of anxiety" has been ubiquitous for more than six decades now.

But is it accurate? As someone who has struggled with chronic anxiety for many years, I have my doubts. For one thing, when you've endured anxiety's insults for long enough — the gnawed fingernails and sweat-drenched underarms, the hyperventilating and crippling panic attacks — calling the 20th century "The Age of Anxiety" starts to sound like calling the 17th century "The Age of the Throbbing Migraine": so metaphorical as to be meaningless.

From a sufferer's perspective, anxiety is always and absolutely personal. It is an experience: a coloration in the way one thinks, feels and acts. It is a petty monster able to work such humdrum tricks as paralyzing you over your salad, convincing you that a choice between blue cheese and vinaigrette is as dire as that between life and death. When you are on intimate terms with something so monumentally subjective, it is hard to think in terms of epochs.

And yet it is undeniable that ours is an age in which an enormous and growing number of people suffer from anxiety. According to the National Institute of Mental Health, anxiety disorders now affect 18 percent of the adult population of the United States, or about 40 million people. By comparison, mood disorders — depression and bipolar illness, primarily — affect 9.5 percent. That makes anxiety the most common psychiatric complaint by a wide margin, and one for which we are increasingly well-medicated. Last spring, the drug research firm IMS Health released its annual report on pharmaceutical use in the United States. The anti-anxiety drug alprazolam — better known by its brand name, Xanax — was the top psychiatric drug on the list, clocking in at 46.3 million prescriptions in 2010.

Just because our anxiety is heavily diagnosed and medicated, however, doesn't mean that we are more anxious than our forebears. It might simply mean that we are better treated — that we are, as individuals and a culture, more cognizant of the mind's tendency to spin out of control.

Earlier eras might have been even more jittery than ours. Fourteenth-century Europe, for example, experienced devastating famines, waves of pillaging mercenaries, peasant revolts, religious turmoil and a plague that wiped out as much as half the population in four years. The evidence suggests that all this resulted in mass convulsions of anxiety, a period of psychic torment in which, as one historian has put it, "the more one knew, the less sense the world made." Nor did the monolithic presence of the Church necessarily help; it might even have made things worse. A firm belief in God and heaven was near-universal, but so was a firm belief in their opposites: the Devil and hell. And you could never be certain in which direction you were headed.

It's hard to imagine that we have it even close to as bad as that. Yet there is an aspect of anxiety that we clearly have more of than ever before: self-awareness. The inhabitants of earlier eras might have been wracked by nerves, but none fixated like we do on the condition. Indeed, none even considered anxiety a condition. Anxiety didn't emerge as a cohesive psychiatric concept until the early 20th century, when Freud highlighted it as "the nodal point at which the most various and important questions converge, a riddle whose solution would be bound to throw a flood of light upon our whole mental existence."

After that, the number of thinkers and artists who sought to solve this riddle increased exponentially. By 1977, the psychoanalyst Rollo May was noting an explosion in papers, books and studies on the subject. "Anxiety," he wrote, "has certainly come out of the dimness of the professional office into the bright light of the marketplace."

None of this is to say that ours is a serene age. Obviously it isn't. It is to say, however, that we shouldn't be possessive about our uncertainties, particularly as one of the dominant features of anxiety is its recursiveness. Anxiety begins with a single worry, and the more you concentrate on that worry, the more powerful it gets, and the more you worry. One of the best things you can do is learn to let go: to disempower the worry altogether. If you start to believe that anxiety is a foregone conclusion — if you start to believe the hype about the times we live in — then you risk surrendering the battle before it's begun.

DANIEL SMITH is the author of the forthcoming book "Monkey Mind: A Memoir of Anxiety" (Simon & Schuster, July 2012). His work has appeared in The Atlantic, Granta, n+1, New York, The New York Times Magazine and elsewhere. He writes regularly about anxiety at his Web site, The Monkey Mind Chronicles.

Ruling Is Victory for Drug Companies in Promoting Medicine for Other Uses

BY KATIE THOMAS | DEC. 3, 2012

IN A CASE THAT could have broad ramifications for the pharmaceutical industry, a federal appeals court on Monday threw out the conviction of a sales representative who sold a drug for uses not approved by the Food and Drug Administration. The judges said that the ban on so-called off-label marketing violated the representative's freedom of speech.

The 2-to-1 decision by a three-judge panel of the Court of Appeals for the Second Circuit in Manhattan addresses a long-running and costly issue for the industry, which has paid billions of dollars in penalties to the federal government in recent years after being accused of marketing blockbuster drugs for off-label uses.

In July, for example, the British drug maker GlaxoSmithKline agreed to pay $3 billion in fines, in part for promoting antidepressants and other drugs for unapproved uses; a month later, Johnson & Johnson announced that its pharmaceutical unit had reached a $181 million consumer fraud settlement with 36 states and the District of Columbia over its marketing of Risperdal, an antipsychotic drug.

"Most if not all of these cases have been based on a central premise: that it is unlawful for a company and one of its employees to be promoting a drug or a medical device off-label," said John R. Fleder, a director at the law firm Hyman, Phelps & McNamara who represented the F.D.A. while working at the Justice Department. "And this decision hits at the heart of the government's theory."

The ruling, in United States v. Caronia, involved the conviction of Alfred Caronia, a former sales representative for Orphan Medical, which was later acquired by Jazz Pharmaceutical. Mr. Caronia was selling Xyrem, a drug approved for excessive daytime sleepiness, known as narcolepsy. He was accused of promoting it to doctors as a treatment for insomnia, fibromyalgia and other conditions. He became the target of a federal investigation in 2005 and was caught on an audiotape discussing the unapproved uses of the drug with a doctor who was a government informant. He was convicted by a jury in 2008.

Mr. Caronia appealed the conviction, arguing that his right to free speech under the First Amendment was being illegally restricted. The appellate court decision applies only to the Second Circuit, which comprises New York, Connecticut and Vermont, but some lawyers said that the government was likely to appeal and that the case could find its way to the Supreme Court.

Under the Food, Drug and Cosmetic Act, which gives the F.D.A. the authority to regulate drugs, selling a "misbranded drug," or one that is intended to be used for purposes not listed in the label, is illegal. Doctors, on the other hand, are free to prescribe a drug for any use. The agency has argued that off-label promotion of drugs is evidence that a sales representative or company intended to sell misbranded drugs.

In its decision, the court said this view violated the First Amendment and cited as precedent a 2011 Supreme Court decision, Sorrell vs. IMS Health. In that case, the high court, citing freedom of speech, overturned a Vermont law restricting pharmaceutical companies from using prescription data for marketing purposes.

"The government clearly prosecuted Caronia for his words — for his speech," the majority wrote, concluding later "the government cannot prosecute pharmaceutical manufacturers and their representatives under the F.D.C.A. for speech promoting the lawful, off-label use of an F.D.A.-approved drug."

The lone dissenting judge, Judge Debra Ann Livingston, vigorously disagreed, arguing that by throwing out Mr. Caronia's conviction "the majority calls into question the very foundations of our century-old system of drug regulation." She argued that if drug companies "were allowed to promote F.D.A.-approved drugs for nonapproved uses, they would have little incentive to seek F.D.A. approval for those uses."

Gerald Masoudi, a former chief counsel of the F.D.A., said the ruling made a distinction between truthful discussion of off-label uses of drugs, many of which are considered legitimate by the medical community, and those that are misleading or false. He noted that "anyone on the planet" could discuss off-label uses of drugs, except for pharmaceutical companies.

"It's very significant," he said, "because it's going to make F.D.A., in its promotion cases, focus on the kinds of speech that are more likely to harm consumers, such as false or misleading marketing versus something that is not approved."

In a statement, the trade group for the pharmaceutical industry, Pharmaceutical Research and Manufacturers of America, said it was pleased with the ruling.

"PhRMA believes that truthful and nonmisleading communication between biopharmaceutical companies and health care professionals is good for patients, because it facilitates the exchange of up-to-date and scientifically accurate information about new treatments," the statement said.

A spokeswoman for the F.D.A. said the agency did not comment on active litigation.

Lawyers said the government would most likely ask for a rehearing before the circuit court's full panel of judges and after that, it could be taken up by the Supreme Court.

Because pharmaceutical companies market their drugs nationally and the ruling applies only within the Second Circuit, the ruling is not likely to lead drug makers to change their marketing policies. Rather, some said, the F.D.A. will be unlikely to pursue convictions in similar cases until the legal issues are resolved.

A.D.H.D. Seen in 11% of U.S. Children as Diagnoses Rise

BY ALAN SCHWARZ AND SARAH COHEN | MARCH 31, 2013

NEARLY ONE IN FIVE high school age boys in the United States and 11 percent of school-age children over all have received a medical diagnosis of attention deficit hyperactivity disorder, according to new data from the federal Centers for Disease Control and Prevention.

These rates reflect a marked rise over the last decade and could fuel growing concern among many doctors that the A.D.H.D. diagnosis and its medication are overused in American children.

The figures showed that an estimated 6.4 million children ages 4 through 17 had received an A.D.H.D. diagnosis at some point in their lives, a 16 percent increase since 2007 and a 41 percent rise in the past decade. About two-thirds of those with a current diagnosis receive prescriptions for stimulants like Ritalin or Adderall, which can drastically improve the lives of those with A.D.H.D. but can also lead to addiction, anxiety and occasionally psychosis.

"Those are astronomical numbers. I'm floored," said Dr. William Graf, a pediatric neurologist in New Haven and a professor at the Yale School of Medicine. He added, "Mild symptoms are being diagnosed so readily, which goes well beyond the disorder and beyond the zone of ambiguity to pure enhancement of children who are otherwise healthy."

And even more teenagers are likely to be prescribed medication in the near future because the American Psychiatric Association plans to change the definition of A.D.H.D. to allow more people to receive the diagnosis and treatment. A.D.H.D. is described by most experts as resulting from abnormal chemical levels in the brain that impair a person's impulse control and attention skills.

While some doctors and patient advocates have welcomed rising diagnosis rates as evidence that the disorder is being better recognized

ROBERT CAPLIN FOR THE NEW YORK TIMES

Dr. Ned Hallowell, a psychiatrist, once told parents some stimulants were "safer than aspirin."

and accepted, others said the new rates suggest that millions of children may be taking medication merely to calm behavior or to do better in school. Pills that are shared with or sold to classmates — diversion long tolerated in college settings and gaining traction in high-achieving high schools — are particularly dangerous, doctors say, because of their health risks when abused.

The findings were part of a broader C.D.C. study of children's health issues, taken from February 2011 to June 2012. The agency interviewed more than 76,000 parents nationwide by both cellphone and landline and is currently compiling its reports. The New York Times obtained the raw data from the agency and compiled the results.

A.D.H.D. has historically been estimated to affect 3 to 7 percent of children. The disorder has no definitive test and is determined only by speaking extensively with patients, parents and teachers, and ruling out other possible causes — a subjective process that is often skipped under time constraints and pressure from parents. It is considered a chronic condition that is often carried into adulthood.

The C.D.C. director, Dr. Thomas R. Frieden, likened the rising rates of stimulant prescriptions among children to the overuse of pain medications and antibiotics in adults.

"We need to ensure balance," Dr. Frieden said. "The right medications for A.D.H.D., given to the right people, can make a huge difference. Unfortunately, misuse appears to be growing at an alarming rate."

Experts cited several factors in the rising rates. Some doctors are hastily viewing any complaints of inattention as full-blown A.D.H.D., they said, while pharmaceutical advertising emphasizes how medication can substantially improve a child's life. Moreover, they said, some parents are pressuring doctors to help with their children's troublesome behavior and slipping grades.

"There's a tremendous push where if the kid's behavior is thought to be quote-unquote abnormal — if they're not sitting quietly at their desk — that's pathological, instead of just childhood," said Dr. Jerome Groopman, a professor of medicine at Harvard Medical School and the author of "How Doctors Think."

Fifteen percent of school-age boys have received an A.D.H.D. diagnosis, the data showed; the rate for girls was 7 percent. Diagnoses among those of high-school age — 14 to 17 — were particularly high, 10 percent for girls and 19 percent for boys. About one in 10 high-school boys currently takes A.D.H.D. medication, the data showed.

Rates by state are less precise but vary widely. Southern states, like Arkansas, Kentucky, Louisiana, South Carolina and Tennessee, showed about 23 percent of school-age boys receiving an A.D.H.D. diagnosis. The rates in Colorado and Nevada were less than 10 percent.

The medications — primarily Adderall, Ritalin, Concerta and Vyvanse — often afford those with severe A.D.H.D. the concentration and impulse control to lead relatively normal lives. Because the pills can vastly improve focus and drive among those with perhaps only traces of the disorder, an A.D.H.D. diagnosis has become a popular shortcut to better grades, some experts said, with many students unaware of or disregarding the medication's health risks.

"There's no way that one in five high-school boys has A.D.H.D.," said James Swanson, a professor of psychiatry at Florida International University and one of the primary A.D.H.D. researchers in the last 20 years. "If we start treating children who do not have the disorder with stimulants, a certain percentage are going to have problems that are predictable — some of them are going to end up with abuse and dependence. And with all those pills around, how much of that actually goes to friends? Some studies have said it's about 30 percent."

An A.D.H.D. diagnosis often results in a family's paying for a child's repeated visits to doctors for assessments or prescription renewals. Taxpayers assume this cost for children covered by Medicaid, who, according to the C.D.C. data, have among the highest rates of A.D.H.D. diagnoses: 14 percent for school-age children, about one-third higher than the rest of the population.

Several doctors mentioned that advertising from the pharmaceutical industry that played off parents' fears — showing children struggling in school or left without friends — encouraged parents and doctors to call even minor symptoms A.D.H.D. and try stimulant treatment. For example, a pamphlet for Vyvanse from its manufacturer, Shire, shows a parent looking at her son and saying, "I want to do all I can to help him succeed."

Sales of stimulants to treat A.D.H.D. have more than doubled to $9 billion in 2012 from $4 billion in 2007, according to the health care information company IMS Health.

Criteria for the proper diagnosis of A.D.H.D., to be released next month in the fifth edition of the Diagnostic and Statistical Manual of Mental Disorders, have been changed specifically to allow more adolescents and adults to qualify for a diagnosis, according to several people involved in the discussions.

The final wording has not been released, but most proposed

changes would lead to higher rates of diagnosis: the requirement that symptoms appeared before age 12 rather than 7; illustrations, like repeatedly losing one's cellphone or losing focus during paperwork, that emphasize that A.D.H.D. is not just a young child's disorder; and the requirement that symptoms merely "impact" daily activities, rather than cause "impairment."

An analysis of the proposed changes published in January by the Journal of Learning Disabilities concluded: "These wording changes newly diagnose individuals who display symptoms of A.D.H.D. but continue to function acceptably in their daily lives." Given that severe A.D.H.D. that goes untreated has been shown to increase a child's risk for academic failure and substance abuse, doctors have historically focused on raising awareness of the disorder and reducing fears surrounding stimulant medication.

A leading voice has been Dr. Ned Hallowell, a child psychiatrist and author of best-selling books on the disorder. But in a recent interview, Dr. Hallowell said that the new C.D.C. data, combined with recent news reports of young people abusing stimulants, left him assessing his role.

Whereas Dr. Hallowell for years would reassure skeptical parents by telling them that Adderall and other stimulants were "safer than aspirin," he said last week, "I regret the analogy" and he "won't be saying that again." And while he still thinks that many children with A.D.H.D. continue to go unrecognized and untreated, he said the high rates demonstrate how the diagnosis is being handed out too freely.

"I think now's the time to call attention to the dangers that can be associated with making the diagnosis in a slipshod fashion," he said. "That we have kids out there getting these drugs to use them as mental steroids — that's dangerous, and I hate to think I have a hand in creating that problem."

ALLISON KOPICKI contributed reporting.

Is It Really A.D.H.D. or Just Immaturity?

BY KJ DELL'ANTONIA | MARCH 11, 2016

NEW RESEARCH SHOWS that the youngest students in a classroom are more likely to be given a diagnosis of attention deficit hyperactivity disorder than the oldest. The findings raise questions about how we regard those wiggly children who just can't seem to sit still — and who also happen to be the youngest in their class.

Researchers in Taiwan looked at data from 378,881 children ages 4 to 17 and found that students born in August, the cut-off month for school entry in that country, were more likely to be given diagnoses of A.D.H.D. than students born in September. The children born in September would have missed the previous year's cut-off date for school entry, and thus had nearly a full extra year to mature before entering school. The findings were published Thursday in The Journal of Pediatrics.

While few dispute that A.D.H.D. is a legitimate disability that can impede a child's personal and school success and that treatment can be effective, "our findings emphasize the importance of considering the age of a child within a grade when diagnosing A.D.H.D. and prescribing medication for treating A.D.H.D.," the authors concluded. Dr. Mu-Hong Chen, a member of the department of psychiatry at Taipei Veterans General Hospital in Taiwan and the lead author of the study, hopes that a better understanding of the data linking relative age at school entry to an A.D.H.D. diagnosis will encourage parents, teachers and clinicians to give the youngest children in a grade enough time and help to allow them to prove their ability.

Other research has shown similar results. An earlier study in the United States, for example, found that roughly 8.4 percent of children born in the month before their state's cutoff date for kindergarten eligibility are given A.D.H.D. diagnoses, compared to 5.1 percent of children born in the month immediately afterward.

So how should we interpret data showing different rates of A.D.H.D. diagnosis among populations of children who are similar in everything other than relative age at school entry? Cautiously, says Michael Manos, the head of Cleveland Clinic Children's A.D.H.D. Center for Evaluation and Treatment.

"The kind of attention that you have to use in school is the kind of attention that's difficult for a person with A.D.H.D.," so attention deficits are more readily recognized in a classroom situation, he said. "If the diagnoses are performed accurately, then some kids are getting noticed sooner than other kids," he said. If younger children with A.D.H.D. are starting treatment earlier because they're starting school earlier, then that's a good thing.

But that presumes the diagnosis is an accurate one. "When you take people who are in a 15-minute pediatric primary care physician's office visit, and the mother describes hyperactivity and the physician automatically prescribes medication, that's a problem," Dr. Manos said. Many parents who describe concerns about children's behavior "aren't describing developmentally inappropriate behavior," he said. "They're describing behavior that does not meet certain expectations," and that can be the issue in classroom settings as well, where some students are older than others.

"I think the link between age at school entry and A.D.H.D. diagnoses are not really about being young or 'not ready,' " said Daphna Bassok, an assistant professor at the University of Virginia's Curry School of Education who has studied kindergarten readiness, by email. "Instead, I think they are about a child's *relative* age."

"In early childhood classrooms, where a month or two age difference can make a big difference," she continued, "teachers perceive the youngest children in the class as having more attention struggles, and behavioral struggles, than the older children, irrespective of the child's actual age." When those teachers flag those struggles, the path to a diagnosis is paved, but the diagnosis itself still depends on the expertise of the clinician.

Stephen Hinshaw, co-author of "A.D.H.D: What Everyone Needs to Know," said that early recognition of attention deficits "could be an opportunity for early intervention for all kindergartners, as our society struggles to balance achievement gaps, ever earlier and stronger achievement expectations, and high student-teacher ratios in Transitional K programs, as well as for evidence-based intervention for 4-year-olds with bona fide A.D.H.D."

"On the other hand, if this is the ticket for overzealous labeling of kids, mainly boys, who are simply needing more time to mature, that's not what we need," Dr. Hinshaw said.

Overselling A.D.H.D.: A New Book Exposes Big Pharma's Role

REVIEW | BY STEVE SILBERMAN | AUG. 22, 2016

ADHD NATION
Children, Doctors, Big Pharma, and the Making of an American Epidemic
By Alan Schwarz
Illustrated. 338 pp. Scribner. $28.

IN THE LATE 1930s, Charles Bradley, the director of a home for "troublesome" children in Rhode Island, had a problem. The field of neuroscience was still in its infancy, and one of the few techniques available to allow psychiatrists like Bradley to ponder the role of the brain in emotional disorders was a procedure that required replacing a volume of cerebrospinal fluid in the patient's skull with air. This painstaking process allowed any irregularities to stand out clearly in X-ray images, but many patients suffered excruciating headaches that lasted for weeks afterward.

Meanwhile, a pharmaceutical company called Smith, Kline & French was facing a different sort of problem. The firm had recently acquired the rights to sell a powerful stimulant then called "benzedrine sulfate" and was trying to create a market for it. Toward that end, the company made quantities of the drug available at no cost to doctors who volunteered to run studies on it. Bradley was a firm believer that struggling children needed more than a handful of pills to get better; they also needed psychosocial therapy and the calming and supportive environment that he provided at the home. But he took up the company's offer, hoping that the drug might eliminate his patients' headaches.

It did not. But the Benzedrine did have an effect that was right in line with Smith, Kline & French's aspirations for its new product: The drug seemed to boost the children's eagerness to learn in the classroom while making them more amenable to following the rules. The drug seemed to calm the children's mood swings, allowing them to become, in the words of their therapists, more "attentive" and "serious," able to complete their schoolwork and behave. Bradley was amazed that Benzedrine, a forerunner of Ritalin and Adderall, was such a great normalizer, turning typically hard-to-manage kids into models of complicity and decorum. But even after marveling at the effects of the drug, he maintained that medication should be considered for children only in addition to other forms of therapy.

Bradley's research was ignored for a couple of decades as psychoanalysis became dominant in the United States. But his discoveries laid the foundation for one of the most aggressive marketing campaigns in history, which succeeded not only in helping to transform the nascent drug industry into the multinational juggernaut known as Big Pharma, but in convincing parents, physicians and public health officials that 15 percent of American schoolchildren are sick enough that they would require powerful medication just to get through the day.

This campaign (which would have horrified Bradley and his peers) is the subject of an important, humane and compellingly written new book called "ADHD Nation," by Alan Schwarz, a reporter for The New York Times. The title of the book, of course, refers to attention deficit hyperactivity disorder: a constellation of behaviors and traits codified as a neurobiological illness in the bible of psychiatry, the Diagnostic and Statistical Manual of Mental Disorders.

The boundaries of the A.D.H.D. diagnosis have been fluid and fraught since its inception, in part because its allegedly telltale signs (including "has trouble organizing tasks and activities," "runs about or climbs in situations where it is not appropriate" and "fidgets with or taps hands or feet," according to the current edition of the DSM) are exhibited by nearly every human being on earth at various points in their development. No blood test or CT scan can tell you if you have the condition — the diagnosis is made by subjective clinical evaluation and screening questionnaires. This lack of any bright line between pathology and eccentricity, Schwarz argues, has allowed Big Pharma to get away with relentless expansion of the franchise.

Numerous studies have shown, for example, that the youngest children in a classroom are more likely to be diagnosed with A.D.H.D. Children of color are also at higher risk of being misdiagnosed than their white peers. One clinician quoted in the book more or less admits defeat: "We've decided as a society that it's too expensive to modify the kid's environment. So we have to modify the kid."

Schwarz has no doubt that A.D.H.D. is a valid clinical entity that causes real suffering and deserves real treatment, as he makes clear in the first two sentences of the book: "Attention deficit hyperactivity is real. Don't let anyone tell you otherwise." But he believes that those who are disabled by the condition deserve a wider range of treatment options than an endless litany of stimulants with chirpy names like Vyvanse and Concerta.

Disorders of attention were once thought to be relatively rare by experts, affecting only an estimated 3 percent of preadolescent children. But kids and teenagers are now diagnosed so routinely that getting a prescription for Ritalin or Adderall has practically become a standard rite of passage, particularly in the United States. And the diagnosis isn't just for children anymore: Its ever-expanding boundaries now encompass allegedly hyperkinetic infants and the distractible elderly. What's really going on?

Influential patient-advocacy groups insist that only now is the true prevalence of A.D.H.D. finally being recognized after being drastically underestimated — akin to the spike in autism diagnoses once the narrowly defined condition was broadened into a spectrum in the 1990s. But Schwarz makes a convincing case that the radical expansion and promotion of A.D.H.D. has resulted in the label being applied in ways that are far beyond the needs of a historically underserved community, while nonpharmaceutical methods of treatment like cognitive behavioral therapy (which have been proved to complement the effectiveness of medication) are overlooked.

While other books have probed the historical roots of America's love affair with amphetamines — notably Nicolas Rasmussen's "On

Speed," published in 2008 — "ADHD Nation" focuses on an unholy alliance between drug makers, academic psychiatrists, policy makers and celebrity shills like Glenn Beck that Schwarz brands the "A.D.H.D. industrial complex." The insidious genius of this alliance, he points out, was selling the disorder rather than the drugs, in the guise of promoting A.D.H.D. "awareness." By bankrolling studies, cultivating mutually beneficial relationships with psychopharmacologists at prestigious universities like Harvard and laundering its marketing messages through trusted agencies like the World Health Organization, the pharmaceutical industry created what Schwarz aptly terms "a self-affirming circle of science, one that quashed all dissent."

In a narrative that unfolds with the momentum of a thriller, he depicts pediatricians' waiting rooms snowed under with pharma-funded brochures, parents clamoring to turn their allegedly underachieving children into academic superstars and kids showered with pills whose long-term effects on the developing brain (particularly when taken in combination) are still barely understood. In one especially harrowing section of the book, Schwarz traces the Icarus-like trajectory of Richard Fee, an aspiring medical student who fakes the symptoms of A.D.H.D. to get access to drugs that will help him cope with academic pressure. When he eventually descends into amphetamine psychosis, his father tells his doctor that if he doesn't stop furnishing his son with Adderall, he'll die. Two weeks after burning through his supply, Fee hanged himself in a closet.

"ADHD Nation" should be required reading for those who seek to understand how a field that once aimed to ameliorate the behavioral problems of children in a broad therapeutic context abdicated its mission to the stockholders of corporations like Shire and Lilly. Schwarz is sounding an alarm for a fire that looks nowhere near abating.

STEVE SILBERMAN is the author of "NeuroTribes: The Legacy of Autism and the Future of Neurodiversity."

A Profusion of Diagnoses. That's Good and Bad.

BY DHRUV KHULLAR, M.D. | NOV. 6, 2018

With millions of Americans taking risky medications for questionable diagnoses, have we medicalized everyday life?

I RECENTLY CARED for a hairdresser who had gone through a year of vague and varied symptoms. What started as a few unpleasant aches soon became debilitating pain throughout her body. A heavy fatigue settled into her bones: Holding scissors or sweeping the floor became too much. She slept fitfully; her memory flagged. Frustrated by many symptoms and few answers, she grew anxious and depressed.

Our medical team, after a battery of unrevealing tests, settled on a diagnosis of fibromyalgia. Tears welled in her eyes as I explained the diagnosis, and I worried I'd been too brusque. But these were tears of relief, she said, not because the symptoms had ceased, but because she finally had an answer, a name for her pain.

Those who suffer without a clear understanding of its cause experience a unique form of torment. There is great power in diagnosis: It can be comforting, terrifying, and sometimes, even healing.

There's evidence, for example, that patients who receive a new diagnosis of fibromyalgia — for which there is limited treatment — may have fewer symptoms, be more satisfied with their health, and possibly incur lower costs.

But fibromyalgia wasn't a recognized diagnosis 30 years ago. Nor were many other now-common diagnoses that have only recently been recognized and treated as medical conditions.

Since the 1980s, there's been rapid expansion in the number and complexity of medical diagnoses — a trend known as "medicalization." A recent study found that the cost of 12 newly medicalized conditions — things like irritable bowel syndrome, post-traumatic stress disorder, low testosterone, attention deficit hyperactivity disorder —

now approaches $80 billion a year, or about 4 percent of total health care spending. That's about as much as we spend on heart disease or cancer, and more than we spend on public health initiatives.

Our ever-expanding armamentarium of diagnoses no doubt offers comfort, attention and a path to treatment for many previously undiagnosed — and undiagnosable — patients. But we may also be medicalizing much of normal human behavior — labeling the healthy as diseased, and exposing them to undue risk of stigma, testing and treatment.

Trouble sleeping is now insomnia. Shyness is social phobia. Grief is depression. Infidelity is sex addiction. It's not that these diseases don't exist — the spectrum of human behavior is broad, and the extremes do represent real pathology — but we may be drawing lines in the wrong places, with negative health and financial consequences.

A central problem is that medicalized diagnoses often come with medicalized treatments: Our penchant for pills outstrips even our desire for diagnosis. Since the 1990s, the number of office visits for sleep problems has doubled, and diagnoses of insomnia have increased sevenfold. But prescriptions for sleep medications have increased more than 30 times.

This is perhaps most concerning for children. About 12 percent of children in America now carry a diagnosis of A.D.H.D, and there was a 40-fold increase in childhood bipolar disorder diagnoses between 1994 and 2003. Five times as many children are now prescribed psychostimulant and antipsychotic medications as were in the 1980s. Today, a quarter of children and teenagers take prescription drugs regularly, and seven percent of older adolescents and young adults report abusing opioids — most of whom were initially prescribed them by a doctor.

With millions of Americans taking risky medications for questionable diagnoses, have we medicalized everyday life?

There's no shortage of factors that have gotten us here. The pharmaceutical industry, for instance, has taken an active, sometimes

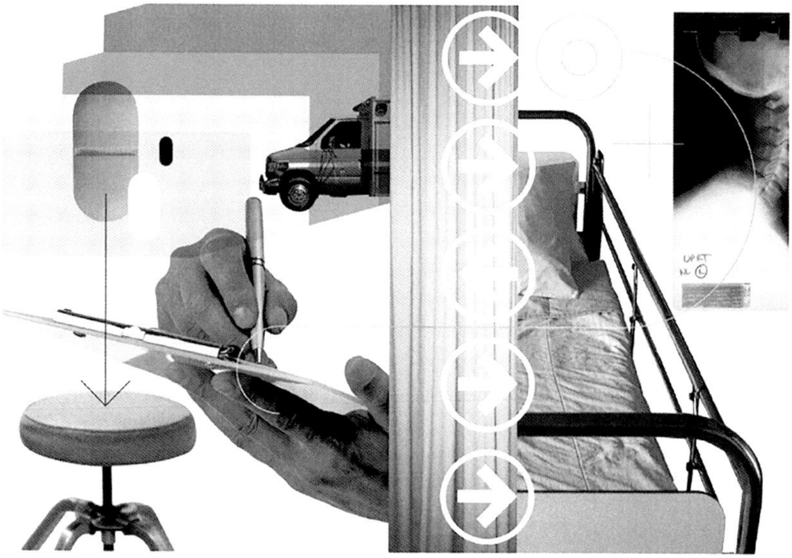

STUART BRADFORD

dubious, role in defining and promoting new diagnoses, through direct-to-consumer advertising and physician outreach efforts.

Often overlooked, however, are how the psychologies of doctors and patients contribute. Clinical encounters that don't end with a definitive diagnosis — a clear acknowledgment of the enemy — are inherently unsatisfying. Doctors, through their training and mandate, are motivated to package a constellation of symptoms into something that can be understood, named and treated. At the same time, we have both a growing arsenal of medications to fix patients' problems and a steadily shrinking number of minutes in which to do so. Not surprisingly, the path of least resistance becomes labeling and prescribing instead of exploring and managing.

Patients are motivated by the understandable desire to name and ease their suffering — and today, many more patients have that opportunity. But it also means that much of normal human experience is treated with prescriptions instead of patience. This is perhaps not surprising. We increasingly have easy solutions at our fingertips: Dial-up modems have given way to broadband; stores are being replaced by Amazon drones; courtship is now Tinder. Is it wrong for patients to expect quick fixes from medicine?

An important step forward may be putting more emphasis on non-prescription remedies. For many medicalized conditions, lifestyle changes are often just as effective as medications, if not more so (and don't come with side effects).

Patients and doctors should also regularly revisit whether a given diagnosis still applies over time. Many patients diagnosed with depression, asthma, acid reflux or insomnia may not meet criteria for these conditions when reassessed, but they often continue taking medications even after symptoms have resolved.

More fundamentally, we need to reconsider where the upper and lower bounds of diagnosis should be. Many experts believe the pendulum has swung too far, such that much of normal human behavior now falls within treatment thresholds. This reassessment is particularly important because those with mild or borderline symptoms may be less likely to benefit from treatment than those with more severe symptoms.

Diagnosis is complicated. It can be a path to acceptance and treatment, or a road to risk and stigma. More diagnoses mean more patients can heal but also that more might suffer. Figuring out who will be helped — and who will harmed — might be the most important diagnosis we make.

DHRUV KHULLAR, M.D., M.P.P. is a physician at NewYork-Presbyterian Hospital, an assistant professor in the departments of medicine and health care policy at Weill Cornell, and director of policy dissemination at the Physicians Foundation Center for Physician Practice and Leadership.

CHAPTER 4

The Money Behind Epidemics: Preventing, Treating and Healing

While modern medicine has made enormous strides within the last century, many diseases are still incurable or impossible to vaccinate against. Pharmaceutical companies push innovation in the face of epidemics — and they can make a lot of money doing it. Today, H.I.V. is considered more manageable than diabetes with medicines that are used preventatively. The N.C.I. funds the development of new and powerful therapies in the war against cancer. And, in the shadow of America's devastating opioid epidemic, drug manufacturers are developing new tamper-resistant therapies to avoid repeating the problems that helped fuel that crisis.

For Profit, Industry Seeks Cancer Drugs

BY ANDREW POLLACK | SEPT. 1, 2009

SAN DIEGO — Pfizer's fortunes in the past were built on cardiovascular drugs, like the cholesterol buster Lipitor and the blood pressure pill Norvasc.

But the future of Pfizer, the world's largest pharmaceutical company, may rest in a cluster of buildings on a bluff not far from the

SANDY HUFFAKER FOR THE NEW YORK TIMES

Jing Yuan, one of 1,000 Pfizer researchers at work at a laboratory in San Diego, developing new drugs to treat cancer.

Pacific Ocean. It is here that Pfizer has amassed about 1,000 researchers for an all-out effort to develop drugs for cancer, a disease the company once largely ignored.

Virtually every large pharmaceutical company seems to have discovered cancer, and a substantial portion of the smaller biotechnology companies are focused on it as well. Together, the companies are pouring billions of dollars into developing cancer drugs.

Two industry trends are driving the push. Recent scientific discoveries have suggested new targets for cancer drug researchers to attack. And as drug companies see profits beginning to wane from mainstays like Lipitor, the high prices that cancer drugs can command have become an irresistible lure.

About 860 cancer drugs are being tested in clinical trials, according to the pharmaceutical industry's main trade group. That is more than twice the number of experimental drugs for heart disease and stroke combined, nearly twice as many as for AIDS and all other infectious diseases combined, and nearly twice as many as for Alzheimer's and all other neurological diseases combined.

But for all the industry's spending and effort, only a trickle of new cancer drugs make it to market. Last year there were two, and this year there has been only one.

And even some of those drugs offer only a few months at most of extra life or tumor stabilization despite prices that often reach thousands of dollars a month. The drug Tarceva, which costs about $3,500 a month, was approved as a treatment for pancreatic cancer because it improved survival by 12 days.

The battle to treat cancer has become, as a commentary in a leading journal put it, a "grinding war of the trenches."

Why? Experts say the same factors that attract drug companies to the cancer business help explain the slow progress.

One reason is scientific. Studies are rapidly revealing the genetic changes in cells that cause cancer and spur its growth. That is providing drug companies with dozens of molecules, or "targets," that drugs could block.

But those same studies have shown that cancer is devilishly complicated. There are so many aberrant molecules in a tumor that blocking just one or two is like trying to stop all traffic in Manhattan with a roadblock at a single intersection.

Tumor cells, like bacteria, can develop resistance to drugs. Some experts believe that drugs that kill most tumor cells do not affect cancer stem cells, which can regenerate the tumor.

And even two people with breast cancer, or two people with lung cancer, might have two very different diseases on the molecular level, so a drug that works for one might not work for the other.

"Cancer is not a single disease," said Robert A. Weinberg, a cancer biologist at the Whitehead Institute and the Massachusetts Institute of Technology. "It's really dozens, arguably hundreds of diseases."

The other reason for the drug makers' interest is financial. Patients are often desperate, and insurers risk outrage by denying payments for a cancer drug, even if the odds say it will have little benefit. That has allowed pharmaceutical companies to charge thousands of dollars a month for cancer medicines. Such prices can make drugs for even rare cancers, or drugs that do not work very well, into big moneymakers.

Take Erbitux, developed by ImClone Systems, which costs $10,000 a month. A study in Canada showed that as a last-ditch treatment for colorectal cancer, Erbitux lengthened lives by an average of about one and a half months compared with not treating the cancer at all. Using the price of the drug in the United States and the average length of treatment, the extra cost per patient was about $50,000.

Erbitux, which is also approved to treat head and neck cancers, recorded global sales of $1.6 billion last year, higher than all but about 70 other drugs. Last year, as part of the industry scramble into cancer drugs, Eli Lilly & Company outbid Bristol-Myers Squibb to acquire ImClone for $6.5 billion.

In 1998, there were only 12 cancer drugs on the list of the world's 200 medicines with the highest sales, compiled by the trade magazine Med Ad News. Taxol, No. 21, was the only cancer drug among the 30 drugs with sales of at least $1 billion.

The same list for last year contained 23 cancer drugs among the top 200 — and three in the top 10. Of the 126 drugs with $1 billion in sales, 20 were for cancer.

Cancer drugs have been the biggest category of drugs in terms of sales worldwide since 2006 and in the United States since 2008, according to the market researcher IMS Health.

Such money attracts companies. "Cancer is such an emotional issue that the free market doesn't work like it does for bicycle wheels and umbrellas," said Robert L. Erwin, a biotechnology industry executive who heads the Marti Nelson Cancer Foundation, a patient advocacy group. "As long as the health care system will pay the price, the money will flow in that direction."

But Mr. Erwin and some other experts say that is not always a good thing for patients because it can set the bar too low for drug companies.

"As long as the marketplace does not distinguish between modestly effective drugs and dramatically effective drugs, there won't be an incentive to shift resources to a greater emphasis on a larger benefit," said Dr. Neal J. Meropol, an oncologist at the University Hospitals Case Medical Center in Cleveland who has been studying drug prices.

Many executives dispute this, saying they would produce drugs offering bigger gains if they knew how. But they must balance their portfolio of experimental drugs between long shots and some drugs that have a better chance of making it to market and sustaining the enterprise.

"If you always swing for home runs, you strike out a lot," said George A. Scangos, chief executive of Exelixis, a biotechnology company with 11 cancer drugs in clinical trials. "It's not the companies' profit motives," he said. "It's largely the difficulty of hitting home runs."

With health care costs rising, there is new pressure on companies to be more selective in drugs they develop. Some experts now talk about "financial toxicity" as a side effect of cancer drug treatment, along with nausea and hair loss.

"A question is how the system can tolerate 400 new drugs on the market, all at the same price" of $50,000 a year, said Dr. Lee Newcomer, senior vice president for oncology at United Healthcare, a big insurer.

Such cost pressures, and the fact that only a handful of cancer drugs get to market each year, mean the big investments now being made into cancer drugs are likely to turn sour for many companies.

"It's the biggest bubble you've ever seen," said Dr. Mark Ratain, an oncologist at the University of Chicago.

But Pfizer is counting on cancer to help save the company. It hopes to reach $11 billion in sales of cancer drugs by 2018. That would be more than four times the category's sales last year of $2.5 billion, which represented only 5 percent of Pfizer's revenue.

Cancer was once unattractive for big pharmaceutical companies like Pfizer. There were relatively few patients with any one type of cancer, and they died fairly quickly. By contrast, there were millions of patients with chronic diseases like hypertension who would take drugs for life.

Indeed, the three main cancer drugs Pfizer now sells came to it with its 2003 acquisition of a rival, Pharmacia, a deal done mainly to acquire the arthritis drug Celebrex.

But there are now many good cardiovascular drugs. Lipitor, the world's best-selling drug, will lose patent protection in 2011, and Pfizer failed to develop a successor.

So Pfizer is scaling back cardiovascular research and has made cancer drugs one of its six focus areas. About 20 percent of Pfizer's more than $7 billion in research and development spending is on cancer, and 22 of the roughly 100 drugs in clinical trials are cancer drugs.

"I've taken a lot of personal interest in this business unit," said Jeffrey B. Kindler, Pfizer's chief executive. "We think we are positioned to be a top leader in oncology."

Cancer research is concentrated here in San Diego, in a cluster of buildings once owned by one of the many biotechnology companies in the region. Pfizer has tried to retain some of the looser culture of entrepreneurial start-ups, like Friday afternoon beer parties. The head of the site, Catherine Mackey, a transplant from Pfizer's laboratories in Connecticut, has become an avid early-morning surfer.

The clinical trials for cancer are being overseen by Dr. Mace L. Rothenberg, an oncologist recruited this year from Vanderbilt University. He hopes Pfizer can develop those home-run drugs. "Having treated patients for 20 years," Dr. Rothenberg said, "I know their needs are not for singles."

The big thrust in cancer drug development for the last few years has been so-called targeted therapies. These drugs aim, so far with modest success, to block aberrant molecules in tumor cells while leaving normal cells unscathed.

But even most targeted therapies have limited impact. One reason is that most tumors are fueled by numerous, often redundant, genetic anomalies. That means that drugs with different targets need to be used in combination. But combinations increase both the costs and side effects of therapy. And it is difficult to test two experimental drugs in combination because the regulatory system is geared to assessing a single drug at a time.

Another reason is that tumors differ among people. Dr. Bert Vogelstein, a cancer geneticist at Johns Hopkins, said a typical tumor might have 50 to 100 genetic mutations. But two patients with the same type of cancer might have only five mutations in common.

So even though a drug might work well for patients whose tumors have a particular mutation, when the drug is used for a broader population, it shows only a small effect.

One solution is to try to determine which patients should get which drug based on the genetic profile of the tumor.

Pfizer is moving in that direction. It plans soon to start a late-stage clinical trial of a drug for lung cancer. But the only patients in the trial will be from the 5 percent or so of lung cancer patients with a mutation in a gene called A.L.K.

"What we're looking for," said Dr. Rothenberg of Pfizer, "is not a small benefit in a large group, but a larger benefit in a smaller group."

For now at least, making the ballpark smaller may be the industry's best chance to hit home runs.

F.D.A. Advisory Panel Backs Preventive Use of H.I.V. Drug

BY DENISE GRADY | MAY 10, 2012

SILVER SPRING, MD. — A drug already used to treat H.I.V. infection should also be approved to prevent it, an advisory panel to the Food and Drug Administration said on Thursday. The recommendation is the first time that government advisers have advocated giving antiviral medicine to healthy people who might be exposed through sexual activity to the virus that causes AIDS.

One panelist called approving the drug "an amazing opportunity to turn the tide on this epidemic."

Studies have shown that people who take the medicine, Truvada, every day have a greatly reduced risk of infection.

The F.D.A. usually accepts the advice of its advisory panels, which are made up of outside medical experts.

On Thursday, after evaluating studies of the once-a-day pill and hearing scientific presentations, the panel recommended that Truvada be prescribed for people at high risk of infection, like gay men who have multiple sex partners, especially those who do not always use condoms, and people in relationships with someone who is H.I.V.-positive. Young black men who have sex with other men are at highest risk. The drug would also be recommended for other high-risk people, like prostitutes.

The drug is meant not to replace condoms and other safe-sex measures, but to be used with them for added protection.

Experts say better methods of prevention are needed because there are 50,000 new H.I.V. infections a year in the United States. Several speakers emphasized Thursday that that number had not budged in 15 to 20 years. Counseling and condoms are not doing the job, they said, and many of the newly infected are men whose sexual partners do not realize they are H.I.V.-positive.

Many panelists voiced concern on Thursday about the possibility that people who become infected while taking Truvada could develop dangerous drug-resistant strains of the virus, but the panel decided that the benefits of preventing new infections outweighed the risks.

An F.D.A. analysis found that people who are older and more educated are more likely to take the drug faithfully. So are men who report having receptive anal sex without condoms. There is no data to tell whether Truvada would prevent H.I.V. infection spread by sharing needles.

Because Truvada has already been approved to treat H.I.V. infection, doctors are free to prescribe it for prevention, and some have been doing so. Prescribing a drug for something other than its approved purpose, called off-label use, is allowed by the F.D.A., though drug companies are not permitted to market or promote drugs for such uses.

Advocates of providing Truvada for prevention say F.D.A. approval would help ensure the drug was more safely and effectively used. The medicine would have to be labeled with specific instructions, including which lab tests patients needed to get for safety reasons. For instance, patients should be tested for H.I.V. infection before starting the drug, because if someone who is already infected takes Truvada alone, drug-resistant strains of the virus may quickly develop. Some patients may also need to have their kidney function checked. And the drug can also cause slight decreases in bone density that may need monitoring in some people.

Despite voting to recommend approval, the panelists struggled with questions about how to make sure that the needed tests are conducted. F.D.A. officials at the meeting argued strongly that there was no practical way for it to enforce a requirement for testing, and that in any case such a requirement would pose too much of a barrier to patients who wanted the preventive drugs.

The voting was not unanimous, and some members of the 22-member panel voted no or abstained because they thought there was not enough data to prove the drug safe and effective in women or black people.

F.D.A. approval may also make it more likely that insurers would cover preventive use, which costs about $14,000 a year.

Truvada, which contains two antiviral drugs, is sold by Gilead Sciences, based in Foster City, Calif. Though it is used alone for prevention, it must be taken along with other antivirals to treat H.I.V. First approved in 2004, it quickly became one of the best-selling H.I.V. drugs. Gilead reported Truvada sales of $758.3 million in the first quarter of this year, which would translate into more than $3 billion a year.

A Gilead official, Dr. Andrew Cheng, told the panel that if Truvada were approved for prevention, the company would conduct safety monitoring and provide educational materials to emphasize the importance of using other prevention methods as well, like condoms, counseling and regular H.I.V. testing. He said Gilead would also provide free condoms and testing for H.I.V. and hepatitis B; subsidized tests for viral resistance for people who become infected; and an assistance program for people with no prescription coverage.

Prevention studies of Truvada have been conducted in the past few years, with somewhat mixed results. A study of 2,499 gay men in six countries, published in 2010, found an overall risk reduction of 44 percent. When researchers looked more closely and checked blood levels of the drug, they found that many of the men had not taken the Truvada pill every day. Among those who did take it correctly, the risk reduction was about 90 percent. But only about 10 percent of the men took the pills exactly as directed.

Some studies in Africa and Asia have also shown significant risk reduction among healthy people whose partners were infected. But other studies in Africa were halted because the drug was showing no benefit in women; subsequent analyses revealed that many of the women were not taking the pills, sometimes because they did not think they were at risk.

The failure of some people in the studies to take the pills every day has led the AIDS Healthcare Foundation, a medical and advocacy group based in Los Angeles, to contend that prescribing Truvada as prevention could backfire, leaving people vulnerable while lulling them into believing that sex without condoms is safe.

"You will definitely have a result that is far worse than what you had in any of the studies," Michael Weinstein, the foundation's president, said in an interview.

But a researcher who conducted the study in gay men, Dr. Robert M. Grant of the Gladstone Institute of Virology and Immunology, which is affiliated with the University of California, San Francisco, disagreed, comparing Mr. Weinstein's argument to that of people in the 1970s who warned that air bags in cars would lead people to stop using seat belts.

"Did that happen?" Dr. Grant asked in an interview. "No."

Matthew Rose, a membership coordinator for the National Lesbian & Gay Journalists Association, described himself to the panel as "a young, H.I.V.-negative black man." He said he and many of his friends were excited about the prospect of a preventive drug.

Growing up gay in Washington, D.C., many young men have their sexual debut at 16 and are H.I.V.-positive by 25, he said, and facing that reality, many want another layer of protection.

"I ask you to give my community another option," Mr. Rose told the panel. "We're not saying it will end the epidemic. But give people options and choices that will work for them, things science tells us will give us a chance."

Advocating Pill, U.S. Signals Shift to Prevent AIDS

BY DONALD G. MCNEIL JR. | MAY 14, 2014

FEDERAL HEALTH OFFICIALS recommended Wednesday that hundreds of thousands of Americans at risk for AIDS take a daily pill that has been shown to prevent infection with the virus that causes it.

If broadly followed, the advice could transform AIDS prevention in the United States — from reliance on condoms, which are effective but unpopular with many men, to a regimen that relies on an antiretroviral drug.

It would mean a 50-fold increase in the number of prescriptions for the drug, Truvada — to 500,000 a year from fewer than 10,000. The drug costs $13,000 a year, and most insurers already cover it.

The guidelines tell doctors to consider the drug regimen, called PrEP, for pre-exposure prophylaxis, for gay men who have sex without condoms; heterosexuals with high-risk partners such as drug injectors or male bisexuals who have unprotected sex; patients who regularly have sex with anyone they know is infected; and anyone who shares needles or injects drugs.

Officials at the Centers for Disease Control and Prevention have long been frustrated that the number of H.I.V. infections in the United States has barely changed in a decade, stubbornly holding at 50,000 a year, despite 30 years of official advice to rely on condoms to block transmission.

Although there is no guarantee that gay men will adopt the drug regimen, federal officials say something must be done because condom use is going down. In a C.D.C. survey in November, the number of gay men reporting recent unprotected sex rose nearly 20 percent from 2005 to 2011.

Nevertheless, advocates for the drug regimen were elated at Wednesday's announcement.

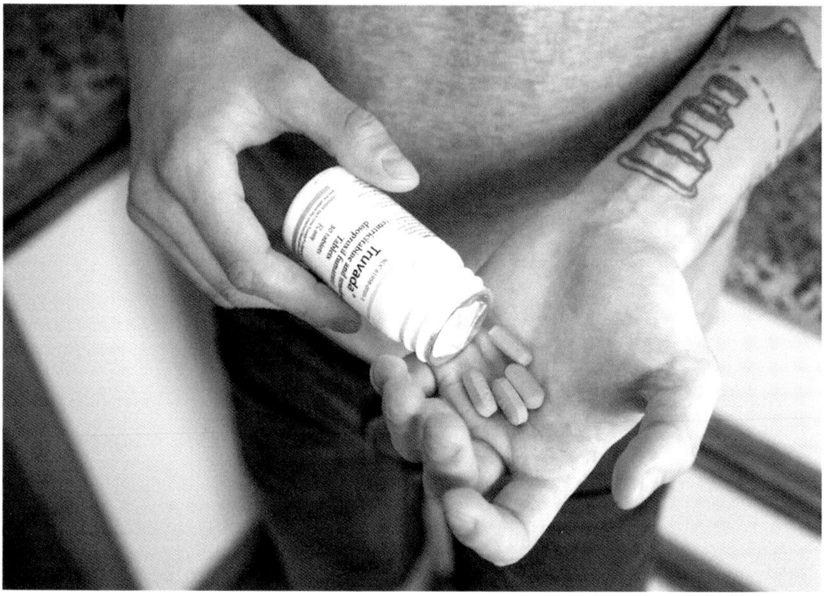

THOR SWIFT FOR THE NEW YORK TIMES

Adam Zeboski takes Truvada, a daily pill that has been shown to prevent infection with the virus that causes AIDS.

"This is wonderful," said Damon L. Jacobs, a therapist in Manhattan who is HIV negative, has been on the regimen since 2011 and runs a Facebook page promoting it. "When an institution like the C.D.C. makes a statement, it makes a profound difference to the doctors who are ambivalent."

Dr. Jonathan Mermin, director of the C.D.C.'s national center for AIDS and other sexually transmitted diseases, said the new guidelines should save many lives.

"On average, it takes a decade for a scientific breakthrough to be adopted," he said. "We hope we can shorten that time frame and increase people's survival."

While many antiretroviral drugs could in theory be used for the drug regimen, the only pill approved for that purpose by the Food and Drug Administration is Truvada, made by Gilead Sciences.

Truvada, a mix of tenofovir and emtricitabine, is considered relatively safe with few side effects. Generic versions are made in India, and it has become the backbone of AIDS treatment in poor countries.

Common side effects include headache, stomach pain and weight loss. Rare but serious ones include liver and kidney damage.

Officially, the C.D.C. is endorsing the drug regimen only in conjunction with condoms. But health officials say they know that some people will stop using them. Many gay men, including Mr. Jacobs, report doing just that.

That raises their risk of contracting other diseases, like syphilis and gonorrhea. But health officials argue that the benefits of taking the drug regimen outweigh the risks.

"Making the perfect the enemy of the good is something we've got to get over," said Dr. Anthony S. Fauci, director of the National Institute of Allergy and Infectious Diseases and the country's best-known AIDS doctor. "I strongly support the C.D.C. doing this."

Syphilis and gonorrhea can usually be cured with antibiotics, but H.I.V. lasts for life and is fatal if left untreated. Even those treated properly often develop early heart disease and other problems.

Since 2010, three separate studies using Truvada have shown that when taken daily it can vastly reduce the chances of infection. That held true for gay men, heterosexual couples and drug injectors. In the study of gay men, known as iPrEx, men whose blood tests showed they had taken their pill every day were 99 percent protected.

The new guidelines say patients should have an H.I.V. test before starting the regimen, to make sure they are not already infected. (Prophylaxis involves doses of two drugs, but anyone with the disease should be on triple therapy.)

Patients should be retested every three months to be sure that they are still H.I.V. negative, that they are not developing side effects from the drug and that they have not caught any other sexually transmitted diseases.

While many AIDS specialists endorse the drug regimen, it has not caught on among doctors as a whole.

A survey of 1,175 infectious disease specialists in the United States and Canada published in December showed that 74 percent supported it, but only 9 percent had actually prescribed it.

"There's a lot of inertia among doctors, and a strong statement from the C.D.C. will be pretty valuable for overcoming that," said Dr. Demetre C. Daskalakis, an AIDS specialist at Mount Sinai Hospital in New York who has many patients on the regimen.

Also, the drug regimen has not caught on among gay men, who are by far the largest risk group.

By analyzing pharmacy databases, Gilead has tried to track how many Truvada prescriptions are for the drug regimen, rather than AIDS treatment. As of last September, the company said, it knew of only 2,319 — of which 49 percent were for women.

Advocates said there were several reasons there had been little clamor for the drug regimen. First, while many doctors prescribe statins as prophylaxis against heart attacks, for example, only AIDS specialists are likely to prescribe AIDS drugs as prophylaxis. But uninfected gay men have no reason to see AIDS specialists, and usually see general practitioners if they see doctors at all.

Also, Truvada is expensive. However, private insurers and state Medicaid programs have thus far generally covered such prescriptions, and Gilead has a program covering co-pays and giving Truvada to the uninsured.

"In my experience, it's a simple process to get the meds approved," Dr. Daskalakis said.

Another reason is that Gilead does not advertise Truvada for prophylaxis, even though the F.D.A. approved it for that use in 2012 and Gilead does advertise it for treatment, for which it was approved in 2004.

A company spokeswoman said it had no plans to do so, but it does make grants to gay organizations that espouse the drug regimen.

Not advertising helps Gilead avoid controversy.

Michael Weinstein, president of the AIDS Healthcare Foundation, has called Truvada a "party drug" and argued that the drug regimen would encourage men to avoid condoms and thus increase the infection rate. He called the release of the guidelines "a shameful chapter in the history of the C.D.C."

That debate has played out on gay websites, where men favoring the drug regimen are often stigmatized as "Truvada whores." (The term was coined in a 2012 Huffington Post article whose author has since publicly regretted his stance.)

"People are reacting out of fear," Mr. Jacobs said. "Gay men who embraced the condom message and survived the trauma of 30 years ago have PTSD. This is a paradigm shift, and people don't like change."

Recently, a lash against the backlash has emerged, with a few men proudly wearing "Truvada Whore" T-shirts, just as others proudly wear "Queer" or "H.I.V. Positive" ones.

Adam Zeboski, a test counselor for the San Francisco AIDS Foundation, makes and sells "Truvada Whore" T-shirts to raise money for the foundation.

"People are both very supportive and very offended," he said. "By reclaiming the 'Truvada Whore' term, we're taking the power away from those who use it against us."

Painkillers Resist Abuse, but Experts Still Worry

BY ALAN SCHWARZ | JUNE 6, 2015

ANTHONY DITULLIO WOULD pop a painkiller in his mouth but not just swallow it, as intended. He would chew it for 30 minutes, grinding through its protective coating and waxy unpleasantness, because the only pain he was treating was addiction.

The pill was OxyContin, a painkiller that its manufacturer, Purdue Pharma, says deters abuse by being difficult to chew or liquefy into forms that give addicts stronger highs, orally or through injection. Since adding these features to its original and widely abused OxyContin in 2010, the company has likened the pill to a virtual seatbelt to restrain the nation's epidemic of prescription drug abuse.

But as thousands of addicts still find ways to abuse OxyContin and similar painkillers, called abuse-deterrent formulations, some experts caution that the protections are misunderstood and could mislead both users and prescribers into thinking that the underlying medications are less addictive.

Because abuse-deterrent formulations are relatively new, preliminary data on their public-health implications is limited. Several studies, some sponsored by Purdue, have found that abuse of OxyContin specifically has decreased after its protections were added. Other reports confirmed those findings but also found that many abusers simply moved on to other opioids, as well as heroin, leaving the overall effect on drug abuse open for debate.

The limitations of abuse-deterrent painkillers were recently underscored when more than 150 residents of southern Indiana contracted H.I.V., the virus that causes AIDS, by sharing needles they used to inject Opana, a drug once marketed as resistant to being liquefied for injection.

"I would definitely say that OxyContin is harder to abuse than it used to be — it was a pain in the neck," said Mr. DiTullio, 35, who

IAN THOMAS JANSEN-LONNQUIST FOR THE NEW YORK TIMES

Anthony DiTullio successfully addressed his painkiller addiction at a drug-treatment facility.

successfully addressed his addiction at a drug-treatment facility and now operates an auto body shop in Keene, N.H. But he added, "No matter what they do, there's always going to be a way for people to get whatever they want in their system."

Nearly two million Americans either abused or were dependent on opioid painkillers in 2013, with 16,000 people dying from overdoses, according to the Centers for Disease Control and Prevention.

Only 1.4 percent of opioid prescriptions filled in 2014 were for abuse-deterrent formulations, according to Express Scripts, the nation's largest prescription-drug manager. More than 219 million prescriptions for opioid painkillers were written in 2014, with sales of $8.85 billion, according to IMS Health, a health care information company.

Three new painkillers were approved last year by the Food and Drug Administration to be marketed as having abuse-deterrent properties. Embeda, from Pfizer, and Targiniq, from Purdue, when crushed release naloxone to counteract the euphoria experienced through snorting or injection. Purdue's Hysingla, like OxyContin, is difficult to chew and liquefy. About 30 more are in development by various companies, according to the F.D.A.

Support for such protections has grown to the point that the agency was roundly criticized in 2013 for going against its advisory committee's recommendation in approving a new painkiller, Zohydro, without deterrent features. (Its manufacturer, Zogenix, has since pursued adding them.) Some lawmakers have pushed for legislation to make the branded drugs cheaper or require that generic versions of older painkillers include abuse-deterrent features.

Dr. Janet Woodcock, the F.D.A.'s director of the Center for Drug Evaluation and Research, has testified that there is a limit to protections that painkillers can carry. "We can't make an impregnable fortress out of the pill," she said in October, "or the patient isn't going to get any pain relief."

Like computer hackers, some drug abusers almost embrace the challenge of cracking abuse-deterrent precautions. (A Purdue executive said last year that two people in its lab "take it personally if they cannot break a formulation.") Websites share various methods, such as microwaving pills or dissolving them in cola overnight.

Opana, made by Endo Pharmaceuticals, proved easy enough to shave into powder or inject that the F.D.A. ruled in 2013 that Endo could no longer call it abuse-deterrent. This has led to some skepticism over whether the formulations live up to their original billing.

"As innovative as the pharmacologic engineers are, the users seem to be just as innovative in their ability to overcome these anti-abuse measures," said Dr. Kevin Burke, a public health officer in the southern Indiana area where Opana abuse caused the recent H.I.V. epidemic. "It's pretty amazing their ability to do that."

Purdue declined requests for an interview, instead providing a statement via email from its chief medical officer, Dr. Gail Cawkwell: "On the whole, society is better off having abuse-deterrent formulations. Focusing solely on what they don't do is like saying seatbelts aren't important because they don't prevent all traffic fatalities. These products won't stop all prescription drug abuse, but they're a necessary part of the solution."

Although technologies can hinder tampering with painkiller pills, the active ingredients in abuse-deterrent drugs provide the same high and remain just as addictive as in regular formulations. Research indicates that the majority of people who abuse or become dependent on prescription opioids do so not by altering the pills but by swallowing them whole.

So even if doctors move toward OxyContin and newer abuse-deterrent formulations, which is roundly supported, many misunderstand the persistent risks, said Dr. G. Caleb Alexander, a co-director of the Center for Drug Safety and Effectiveness at the Johns Hopkins Bloomberg School of Public Health.

A national survey of internists, family physicians and general practitioners that Dr. Alexander led last year found that about one-third of them incorrectly thought that most prescription opioid abuse is non-oral. More worrisome, he said, almost half of those doctors thought that abuse-deterrent pills were inherently less addictive. A paper based on the survey is being reviewed by a scientific journal.

"Prescribers don't appreciate what these formulations do and what abuse-deterrent actually means," Dr. Alexander said. "They overestimate the safety of these products. With a term like abuse-deterrent, how can't it be the best thing since sliced bread?"

Because of this, the products should be called only "tamper-deterrent," said Bob Twillman, the executive director of the American Academy of Pain Management. But the F.D.A. already uses the term "tamper-resistant" to describe outside packaging only.

Some experts are also wary that, given some manufacturers' history of understating the dangers of opioids, they could be overstating their protective measures as well. In 2007, Purdue was fined more than $600 million, and three of its executives pleaded guilty to individual criminal charges, for misrepresenting OxyContin's risks for addiction.

The C.E.O. of H.I.V.

BY CHRISTOPHER GLAZEK | APRIL 26, 2017

Michael Weinstein's AIDS Healthcare Foundation treats an enormous number of patients — and makes an enormous amount of money. Is that why so many activists distrust him?

LAST MAY, AT THE height of the Democratic presidential campaign, two weeks before the California primary, Bernie Sanders flew to San Bernardino, Calif., for a meeting with leading AIDS groups. The gathering was arranged by Peter Staley, the esteemed activist and founder of the Treatment Action Group, which in the 1990s helped speed the development of antiretroviral drugs. The meeting was called to secure the Sanders campaign's support for a spike in federal spending to combat AIDS, but as the session began, those in attendance were puzzled to find the conversation oddly strained. Sanders's demeanor, Staley recalled, "was very wary — he was very chilly when we shook hands." Sanders seemed to be churning internally about something until, dispensing with ceremony, he blurted out: "Let me be blunt. Do any of you get money from the drug companies?"

The question was met with an awkward silence. Most AIDS organizations do accept grants from pharmaceutical companies — in some cases large ones. It is widely seen as a symbiotic relationship. AIDS nonprofits depend on funding from drug companies; drug companies depend on the organizations to educate patients about their wares. That arrangement rankled Sanders, who views the pharmaceutical industry as a public menace. In the primary, one of his signature issues was support for California's Proposition 61, a referendum that sought to control drug prices by barring public insurers from paying any more than the prices charged to the Veterans Health Administration, which traditionally gets a big discount. A few of the AIDS activists gathered in San Bernardino — along with a number of experts and patient groups — had strong reservations about the unintended consequences of that initiative. Some worried it would drain R.&D. budgets; others feared it would prod drug companies to jack up prices on veterans. Sanders did not share their reservations about Prop. 61. "Drug companies are ripping off the American people in a big way," he said. "These are bad-news people, and they need to be taken on."

The next day, the Sanders campaign circulated a news release about the meeting, which, to Staley's shock, focused entirely on Sanders's support for Prop. 61, and, in Staley's view, gave the misleading impression that everyone present joined Sanders in endorsing the referendum. After Staley took to Facebook to dispute the account — "Feeling used and abused by the Sanders campaign right now," he wrote to 12,000 followers — the Sanders campaign's policy director, Warren Gunnels, attacked Staley personally on Twitter. Using scare quotes to insinuate that Staley, who once chained himself to a balcony of the New York Stock Exchange to protest high drug prices, didn't really deserve to be called an "activist," Gunnels claimed that Staley had "made a fortune from big drug companies." As evidence, Gunnels linked to a post on a website called Stop Pharma Greed that was teeming with opposition research on some of the biggest names in AIDS activism. The post accused Staley of "shilling for big Pharma" and taking funding from companies like DuPont Pharmaceuticals, GlaxoSmithKline and Gilead Sciences. "In short," the post concluded, "Staley's livelihood since the year 2000 ... appears to have been wholly dependent on, or funded directly by, the drug industry." Staley called the accusation a "Trumpian lie," noting that he has lived entirely on savings for the last five years. (The tweet was later deleted.)

The activists hadn't known what to make of Sanders's frostiness, but as soon as they saw Gunnels's tweet, the fog lifted. Staley believed that someone had goaded the Sanders campaign into going nuclear on him, and he had no doubt about who that someone was. Stop Pharma Greed was funded by Staley's longtime nemesis, Michael Weinstein, the 64-year-old founder and director of the AIDS Healthcare Foundation, the world's largest and most controversial AIDS organization.

(The Sanders campaign denied Staley's claim.) Weinstein was also the financier behind Prop. 61, which would go on to become the most expensive referendum of 2016, thanks to the pharmaceutical industry, which spent $120 million on the campaign, and eventually defeated it with 53 percent of the vote. More money was spent against Prop. 61 than was spent on behalf of any candidate for governor or Senate in 2016.

Directors of health care nonprofits are traditionally cautious and courtly, fearful of choking the funding streams that issue from nit-picking grant committees and image-conscious donors. Weinstein, an ex-Trotskyite, is no courtier. He runs his organization as a "social enterprise," meaning that it generates most of its revenue not from grants and fund-raising but from adjacent businesses. A.H.F.'s main business is a network of pharmacies and clinics that provide primary care to more than 41,000 patients in the United States, most of whom have their insurance claims paid by government insurance programs like Medicaid. The excess income from these patients helps the AIDS Healthcare Foundation provide free care to more than 700,000 H.I.V. patients internationally — the greatest reach of any AIDS organization. This prodigiously successful model has both insulated A.H.F. from typical funding woes and helped it to expand at an astonishing clip. Over the last six years, A.H.F.'s budget has grown from $300 million to more than $1.4 billion, about the size of Planned Parenthood. If their projections hold, it will reach $2 billion by 2020, giving A.H.F. — a private entity effectively under the control of one man — a budget nearly half the size of the World Health Organization's.

Paradoxically, that projected growth depends in part on whether drug costs remain high. While cutting drug prices is an ideological objective for Weinstein, his pharmacies stand to lose revenue should he succeed in that mission. "Most of the time when people benefit from something, they don't lobby against it," he told me recently. "But we're Robin Hood. If someone was writing an epitaph for this organization some day, it will be: 'Bit the hand that fed it.' "

A.H.F.'s rapid ascent has made Weinstein an object of scorn among his peers, who deplore not only his tactics but also his unorthodox positions on public-health issues. Unlike nearly all other AIDS activists and public-health researchers, Weinstein opposes PrEP, the H.I.V.-prevention pill, which he believes will cause a "public-health catastrophe" by triggering a dangerous increase in risky sex. He has also campaigned to make condoms mandatory in adult films, even going so far as to introduce a statewide referendum in California, Proposition 60. Weinstein's positions have been assailed by peers as counterproductive fearmongering. "It reminds me very much of the Tea Party people with regard to Obamacare," Ernest Hopkins, director of legislative affairs for the San Francisco AIDS Foundation, told me in 2013, referring to Weinstein's opposition to PrEP. "If you're prepared to say whatever you want and lie and demagogue and misrepresent the facts, then you can get a lot of airtime, and you can also persuade a lot of people."

To his many critics in AIDS activism, Weinstein is the Koch brothers of public health: a mastermind driven by ideology, accountable to no one, with bottomless funds and an agenda marked by financial opportunism and puritanical extremes. It doesn't help that A.H.F. has been the subject of near-constant litigation and complaints for questionable business practices, including union-busting, giving kickbacks to patients, overbilling government insurers and bullying funders into denying grants to institutional rivals. (A.H.F. has denied these accusations.)

To his faithful, however, Weinstein is not only a provider of superior health care but also an evangelist of moral urgency at a time when prevention efforts are floundering and drug prices are surging. Weinstein seems to view himself in loftier terms, as a holy warrior sent to save the innocent, not only from the scourge of H.I.V. but also from those he views as the virus's human collaborators: a satanic trifecta of greedy executives, vainglorious activists and incompetent bureaucrats.

WEINSTEIN'S OFFICE, a cold and tidy room overlooking the Hollywood Hills, is an archive of sentimental zealotry. On his desk, an outward-facing plaque greets visitors with a defiant warning attributed to Hannibal — "I shall either find a way or make one," a reference to herding war elephants over the Alps to destroy Rome. On one wall, a framed resolution from the California State Legislature honoring Weinstein for his community service hangs incongruously beside an orphaned sheet of paper printed with a Harry Truman-ism: "It's amazing what you can accomplish when you do not care who gets the credit." Above the Truman quotation, there's a photo of Weinstein in front of the Taj Mahal, sitting alone in a red shirt; there are no photos of Weinstein's husband, a Vietnamese immigrant who owns a nail salon. A second piece of Scotch-taped paper bears an aphorism of Weinstein's own coinage: "Help Defeat Self-Imposed Helplessness."

The first time I visited, in February of last year, Weinstein invited me to sit down without shaking my hand. A lean man with a long forehead, bird-of-prey features and a nerdy, pocket-protector vibe, Weinstein had a formal demeanor but was wearing jeans and a hoodie — a common outfit for a tech leader but unusual for a health care magnate. Weinstein took me on an abbreviated tour, proudly showing off photos he had taken with celebrities and political figures — Magic Johnson, Alicia Keys, former Senator Tom Harkin. Above his desk hung an Expressionist portrait of his best friend, with whom he founded A.H.F., Chris Brownlie. By all accounts, Brownlie was the softhearted yin to Weinstein's gladiatorial yang, as charming and consensus-seeking as Weinstein was splenetic and introverted. Brownlie died from AIDS-related complications in 1989.

Weinstein has a long history of militancy. Born in Brooklyn's Bensonhurst neighborhood to a family of left-wing Jews, at age 13 he volunteered for an antiwar congressional candidate and worked as an equipment mule for his filmmaker sister, toting around a 40-pound battery while she shot footage of protesters burning draft cards in Central Park. The next year, he joined a group of activists occupying a new high-rise development to protest what was not yet known as gentrification. Though he realized he was gay early on, he repressed his sexuality for many years, eventually moving in with an older girlfriend. At age 18, he had his first gay encounter with an upstairs neighbor, also officially straight, who knocked on his door one night when both of their girlfriends were out of town.

In 1972, when Weinstein was 19, he traveled to California and joined Los Angeles's gay activism scene. An outsider among both mainstream gays (for being a Marxist) and Marxists (for being gay), Weinstein decided to start his own group, which he called the Lavender and Red Union. The group eventually merged with a gay-friendly Trotskyite organization in New York called the Spartacist League, which offered Weinstein a leadership position, requiring him to move back to the East Coast. He wasn't at his new post for long, though, before he fell out with his comrades over an unusual matter: the Roman Polanski sexual-abuse case, in which the director was accused of drugging and raping a 13-year-old girl. "They felt that it was not rape, that the girl knew what she was doing," Weinstein's boyfriend at the time, Albert Ruiz, told me. Weinstein believed it was rape and felt strongly enough about the matter, among other disputes, that he resigned.

Disillusioned with activism, Weinstein briefly ran a candy business in Los Angeles before returning to politics to face an unlikely antagonist. In 1986, the right-wing conspiracy theorist Lyndon LaRouche introduced a ballot referendum in California that would have enabled employers to fire people with AIDS and empowered the government to quarantine them. Early polling suggested that LaRouche's initiative had broad support. Along with Brownlie and other friends, Weinstein started his own group to fight LaRouche's proposition. In a move that anticipated his later shock-marketing campaigns, Weinstein distributed leaflets with the headline "STOP AIDS CONCENTRATION CAMPS" and organized a torch-lit march on LaRouche's Silver Lake office. Mainstream gay activists abhorred Weinstein's strong-arm tactics, fearing he might alienate suburban voters. But after the measure lost in a landslide, with 71 percent opposed, L.A. Weekly named Weinstein "Best Young

Activist." Weinstein determined that there was far greater support for his militant approach than he had realized.

As the AIDS crisis intensified, Weinstein watched more and more of his friends grow ill and die. Los Angeles County hospital had barely developed procedures for handling dying AIDS patients, and many were left to expire alone on gurneys in crowded hallways. Doctors and nurses would often refuse to care for AIDS sufferers, and when the untreated patients died, undertakers often turned them away, too. In some parts of the country, the deceased ended up in garbage bags delivered directly to crematories. Weinstein wanted to ensure that AIDS patients could die in a respectful, peaceful atmosphere. In 1989, he and Brownlie founded the precursor of A.H.F. — the AIDS Hospice Foundation. In 1990, as more AIDS medications became available, Weinstein changed the group's name to the AIDS Healthcare Foundation and shifted its focus to medical care for the living. In the late '90s, little by little, A.H.F. expanded from Southern California into Florida and New York. Then, in 2000, A.H.F. made a change that would prove crucial to its business model: It opened its first pharmacy.

Pharmacy services are, in Weinstein's words, A.H.F.'s "jet fuel." That's because 70 percent of spending on H.I.V. care consists of drug costs. While H.I.V. patients in the United States skew poor, the costly insurance claims they generate by filling prescriptions make them gold mines, not only for pharmaceutical companies but also for certain pharmacies, like Weinstein's, that take advantage of a federal program called 340B. Passed in 1991, 340B allows pharmacies attached to medical practices serving underprivileged populations to buy drugs directly from manufacturers at, on average, a 35 percent discount but still be reimbursed by insurers for 100 percent of the wholesale price. In effect, 340B allows pharmacies to keep around 35 percent of the pharmaceutical industry's tab, a roundabout way of subsidizing health care for the poor. As the price of AIDS medications has spiraled upward in recent years, A.H.F.'s coffers have swelled. The cost of the latest first-line H.I.V. treatment — a combination pill from Gilead called Genvoya —

is about $34,000 per patient per year. When a patient uses an A.H.F. pharmacy, about $22,000 of that bill goes to Gilead, and $12,000 goes to A.H.F. The foundation's pharmacies serve 50,000 patients in the United States, generating approximately $1 billion each year in revenue — about $200 million of it surplus. That money subsidizes A.H.F.'s expansion and advocacy as well as the group's political activities.

The pool of potential patients for an organization like A.H.F. is oceanic. In 2014, 37,600 Americans were newly infected with H.I.V. That number has declined only slightly over the last decade, as America's epidemic has settled into a baleful equilibrium of slow growth and rising costs. The lack of progress is especially disheartening considering that H.I.V. medications, when properly administered, render patients almost totally noninfectious. These medications aren't new — they've existed for two decades. If every infected American took them, our epidemic would be over. Instead, of the roughly 1.2 million Americans with H.I.V., only 40 percent are on medication, a rate lower than South Africa's. Weinstein believes that America's AIDS nonprofits, which he refers to derisively as "AIDS Inc." — a label meant to evoke sclerotic incumbents who collect renewable grants and stand only for their own perpetuation — have been useless in the face of the epidemic. To win, he thinks, "AIDS Inc." has to be sidelined so that A.H.F. can lead the way.

LAST SPRING, WEINSTEIN summoned 30 foot soldiers to the Sheraton Hotel in New Orleans for a retreat for A.H.F.'s sales team — a division that doesn't exist at most nonprofits because most nonprofits have nothing to sell. A.H.F. does: It sells health care to a customer base overwhelmingly composed of patients receiving government assistance, and each new patient it acquires means more cash for its operations. The sales team at A.H.F. is responsible for recruiting new patients, a function they perform by scouring homeless shelters, hosting parties at gay clubs, cozying up to local clinicians and deploying mobile-testing vans to H.I.V. hot spots. It's a commissions-driven gig. For each new patient who goes to an A.H.F. clinic and fills an antiretroviral prescription at an A.H.F. pharmacy, the rep receives $300. He or she receives an additional $300 when patients fill their prescriptions a second time — the second fill being a more reliable predictor of patient retention.

To recruit new patients, sales reps are expected to hold several events each month, most of them in high-risk zones. Events vary by location. On Los Angeles's Skid Row, for example, reps hand out McDonald's gift cards to anyone willing to take a rapid H.I.V. test. In South Central, the reps sometimes set up a game called Cash Box, in which contestants who agree to a rapid test enter a plexiglass booth where they try to grab cash as it is blown around at high speeds. In gay neighborhoods, reps may invite passers-by to play Dildo Toss — a carny-inspired game in which players hurl phalluses of varying colors and sizes into a hole carved out of a plank of wood. "We give them three chances," explained Edwin Millan, director of sales for the Western United States, "and if it goes in the hole, they get to spin a wheel and they get a prize." (In 2015, two former employees filed a whistle-blower suit arguing that A.H.F.'s patient incentives amounted to illegal kickbacks; the lawsuit has not yet reached a resolution, and A.H.F. denies the claims.) In addition to seeking out patients directly, sales reps also cultivate referral sources by hosting lunches for area doctors.

The retreat's kickoff dinner was held in the French Quarter, at Deanie's Seafood. Tucked away in a back room, the gregarious sales reps kibitzed noisily, slurping crawfish étouffée as Weinstein, seated at the head of a long table, examined his battalion. Like other divisions at A.H.F., this group was anchored by black women in floral prints and gay men of all races in checkered shirts; many were new hires Weinstein was meeting for the first time. "Sometimes I have to pinch myself," Weinstein whispered to me, marveling at how swiftly his organization had expanded.

As the sales reps emptied their plates and hailed waiters for second and third rounds of wine, Weinstein tapped his glass with a fork and called the group to attention. "I'd like to officially welcome you to the Big Easy!" he squawked in his blunt Brooklynese. "Do whatever you want as long as you wake up in the morning." The reps laughed. "You know, this is a really powerful force on behalf of the organization — a powerful force on behalf of the growth. Going out there, pounding the pavement, going after new accounts and clients — you have to be immune to rejection to be successful, and that's not easy. I'm pretty bad at it myself!" He wasn't kidding. Weinstein belies the cliché that the best fighters develop a thick skin: He has sustained himself through decades of conflict by salting unhealed wounds, nursing unceasing resentment and preserving grudges in amber.

The morning after the dinner, the sales reps reconvened in a dreary conference room with red tablecloths and damask carpeting. Programming for the first day called for an icebreaker in which employees were asked to scribble unusual facts about themselves on pieces of paper tossed into a hat. One man, a bodybuilder from South Beach with silver hair and pumpkin-colored skin, wrote that he used to train with Madonna; a copper-haired woman from San Francisco disclosed that she swam through garbage during an initiation ritual for Semester at Sea. Weinstein's own fact, the one he always uses for such exercises, was that he dropped out of high school.

The icebreaker was followed by an exercise intended to explore how to navigate conversations with A.H.F.'s critics. Weinstein gave volunteers the option of representing the San Francisco AIDS Foundation, leaders of which have been vocally critical of A.H.F., or a "PrEP crazy," someone incensed by Weinstein's opposition to the H.I.V.-prevention pill. Another volunteer would play A.H.F.

"I'll be S.F.A.F.!" volunteered the copper-haired woman. Her counterpart was a man whose upper lip was adorned with a sumptuous mustache.

"I'm here to talk to you about the services that we provide," he began.

"I know all about A.H.F., actually," replied the copper-haired woman, her eyes narrowing. "Your reputation precedes you."

"O.K., awesome. Did you know that we started the first AIDS hospice in Los Angeles about 28 years ago?" he asked. "Since then, we've grown rapidly, primarily overseas."

"I know you've grown rapidly," she snapped, summoning a glower. "You're the Walmart of H.I.V." She went on: "I've been in the H.I.V. field for 30 years! I've lived through the epidemic; I've seen all my friends die. You guys advertise yourselves as this 'not-for-profit.' I know the true thing: You guys are a huge profit source. I can't even find your financials on your website — you hide those."

The reps laughed; they'd all heard some version of this tirade a thousand times. Weinstein took the floor and concluded the session by telling a little story about a nun he once met. She ran a hospital, which required her to make tough budgetary decisions in the name of helping people. Whenever people criticized her for being harsh, she had a canned response: "No margin, no mission!" This, according to Weinstein, is what A.H.F.'s critics couldn't bring themselves to understand. "We should never be in a position of apologizing for our success," he said. "The fact that we take a business model from the private sector and utilize it on behalf of a nonprofit is a great thing."

THIS SAINTLY NARRATIVE is complicated by the fact that Weinstein has drawn from his plentiful war chest to underwrite a dizzying number of controversial projects, some of which seem only tenuously connected to his core mission. In addition to the drug-pricing initiative and the condoms-in-porn bill, he filed a lawsuit against Gilead Sciences, the leading manufacturer of AIDS drugs, for patent manipulation (Gilead prevailed in court; A.H.F. has filed an appeal). He led a petition drive in Mississippi to remove Confederate symbols from the state flag, and he funded an anti-density campaign in Los Angeles that sought to halt construction on most new residential towers for two years, including a 28-story project across the street from Weinstein's global headquarters.

And then there are the billboards. In major American cities — and increasingly, around the world — Weinstein's most visible impact is his trolling approach to sexual-health messaging. In 2013, he put up signs in several cities with the image of a magma-spewing volcano captioned, "SYPHILIS EXPLOSION." The following year, in South Central, he posted billboards with two black men spooning in bed alongside the leading question "Trust Him?" Some ads have been humorous and topical — a sendup of the Netflix logo replaced with the mantra "Get Tested and Chill," a Bernie Sanders parody with the modified slogan "Feel the Burn?" Others have hectored the public with reproachful questions: "Friends With Benefits?" "Sexually Reckless?" "Worried?" One A.H.F. billboard managed to cause a national scandal in Uganda. Unusually for a nonprofit, A.H.F. employs a 15-person in-house creative agency to create its messaging. The expense is justified because the billboards are a marketing channel: They seek to stir dread in the libertine masses, not only to stem what Weinstein sees as a rising tide of promiscuity but also to drive traffic to his clinics.

In the press, Weinstein has attracted the most attention for his hostility to PrEP, a once-a-day antiretroviral that reduces the likelihood of contracting H.I.V. by 99 percent. In 2015, the C.D.C. began recommending PrEP for anyone at "high risk" for H.I.V. infection, including any gay man not in a monogamous relationship who has had sex in the last six months without a condom (1.2 million people, according to the C.D.C.'s estimates). Many hailed it as an era-defining advance. Weinstein, virtually alone among major AIDS figures, has assailed PrEP, calling it a "party drug" that could lead to a collapse in condom use. In a citizen petition to the Food and Drug Administration following PrEP's approval in 2012, A.H.F.'s lawyer denounced the treatment as "unsafe and ineffective." Weinstein called on Margaret Hamburg, the agency's commissioner, to resign over the issue, suggesting she was part of a pharma-led plot to put millions of Americans on a new medication.

Weinstein's critique of PrEP is a fringe view. According to Anthony Fauci, director of the National Institute for Allergy and Infectious Diseases, support for PrEP among researchers and regulators is all but universal. "It's having an extraordinarily positive impact," he says.

Robert Grant, a professor of medicine at U.C.S.F. and a leading PrEP researcher, credits the treatment with "a plummeting decline" in H.I.V. transmission rates among white gay men in San Francisco.

Nevertheless, Weinstein is quoted regularly in articles about the treatment, and his noisy skepticism has reverberated across the internet. Some argue that Weinstein's grandstanding during public hearings delayed PrEP's approval by the C.D.C., and that his sowing of doubt about the medication is continuing to suppress its use, especially in black and Latino communities. "What I find in my practice," Grant says, "is that A.H.F.'s propaganda does not impress or influence privileged groups of gay men. They can see right through it. But when I talk to some people of color who are clients in my clinics, I find they've heard the A.H.F. message, and it gives them pause, it makes them concerned, it appeals to their sense that this isn't for them." Despite the C.D.C.'s efforts, very few people, even now, are on PrEP; according to recent estimates, only about 100,000 people take it.

Weinstein's concerns about PrEP are in line with his other heterodox positions, which often cut against the sexual-liberationist doctrine embraced by other activists. Many issues that have been controversial in the gay community, he claims, like laws that make it illegal to intentionally infect a sexual partner with H.I.V., are no-brainers for ordinary voters. "Some people are so extreme," he told me. "There's a group here in California that wants to reduce intentionally infecting somebody from a felony to a misdemeanor. There's articles being written basically saying we should be proud to bareback" — slang for condomless sex. "In the hothouse environment of the gay community, that point of view is very popular, but it isn't in the community at large, and it isn't in the medical community either."

What motivates Weinstein to adopt such lonely views? Weinstein's fiercest critics have often searched for a financial motive, some even going so far as to suggest that he aims to profit from the spread of H.I.V. Those who know him personally dismiss this explanation. Phill Wilson, president of the Black AIDS Institute, first met Weinstein in

1980 when Wilson was dating Chris Brownlie. In fact, the first iteration of A.H.F. was founded in Wilson's living room. "This is the mistake that people make when they think about Michael," Wilson told me. "Whether what he does is good or bad, he does what he believes is in the best interests of people living with H.I.V. or at risk of infection." Weinstein was "primarily driven by mission," Wilson said. Even Peter Staley concedes that point. "I don't think it's about the money for him," he told me, unsurprised to learn that in Weinstein's most recent annual report, he disclosed a comparatively humble salary of $400,000, low for directors of similarly sized nonprofits. "The core of the business at A.H.F. is not something that has been scandalous," Staley says. "It is an empire worth building. A.H.F.'s problem is that once it created the largest AIDS empire on the planet, it started using that power for nefarious purposes: Michael Weinstein's twisted political views."

ON PAPER, 2016 was Weinstein's best year ever. He opened six new pharmacies and one clinic in the United States and started new programs in Indonesia, Bolivia and Zimbabwe. But on the advocacy side, he suffered significant setbacks. In November, his drug-pricing initiative failed. So did his condoms-in-porn initiative, despite the fact that he had managed to pass a similar law in Los Angeles County in 2012. Most recently, on March 7, voters in the city of Los Angeles resoundingly rejected, by a 2-to-1 margin, his quixotic anti-density measure. The public, it seems, is not on board with Weinstein's agenda.

Even so, when I visited Weinstein at his office in February, he showed no sign of disappointment. Discussing recent losses, he wasn't merely philosophical; he was downright giddy. "I had never been involved with a campaign," he said, referring to the drug-pricing initiative, "where people were so enthusiastic about something that didn't win." (He would later use the same line with reporters when his anti-density ordinance went down in flames.) As we chatted, he sipped from a radioactive-looking bottle of apple-melon Isopure; he said he liked his chances for this November, when he would try again with a new drug-pricing initiative, this time in Ohio. The problem in California, he said, was that the drug companies had flooded the airwaves — "total aerial bombardment, 3,500 gross rating points a week" — but he doubted that kind of "razzmatazz" would work in flyover country. "Midwesterners are kind of square-shouldered, common-sense people. I'd think there'd be a backlash if they dumped $80 million into Ohio."

If that referendum were to pass, Weinstein figured, then Big Pharma's citadel — the American market — would start to crack. Ohio would be copied by other states, and the V.A.'s price for drugs would become the universal price, as even private insurers would demand to pay the new public rate. Billions would be shaved off pharma's bottom line, meaning the industry would no longer have the muscle to bully Congress into propping up its international patent regime. Drug prices would plummet across the world, AIDS medications would flow freely and the industry's lobbying operation would shrink so much that it could be drowned in a bathtub. This sequence of events seemed far-fetched, but Weinstein was nevertheless optimistic about the coming year, win or lose. His equanimity in the face of failure reminded me of something he once said to me about Prop. 60, the condoms-in-porn bill. It lost at the ballot box by an eight-point margin, but Weinstein found a reason to declare victory. "We've had more than 10,000 stories on condoms in porn," he boasted. "Forget about porn: That's a lot of free advertising for condoms."

Weinstein often consoles himself in moments of defeat by reaffirming his commitment to the long game. This is part of what makes him so frustrating to his critics: It is difficult, and sometimes impossible, to distinguish his cynical ploys from his ideological commitments. In his person, the will to power and the will to change the world seem to fuse. It wasn't simply that he cared more about fighting than about winning. Eventually, he believes, people will come around to his view. And if they don't, that's fine, too: A.H.F. will continue to thrive, even in a fallen world

CHRISTOPHER GLAZEK is a freelance writer based in New York and the founder of the Yale AIDS Memorial Project.

The Insanity of Taxpayer-Funded Addiction

EDITORIAL | BY THE NEW YORK TIMES | NOV. 10, 2017

THE PHARMACEUTICAL INDUSTRY was listed as one of the "Contributors to the Current Crisis" in the final report of President Trump's Commission on Combating Drug Addiction and the Opioid Crisis. The report cites decades of aggressive marketing and industry-sponsored physician "conferences" aimed at expanding opioid use by minimizing the dangers of addiction. Lawsuits by state attorneys general, counties and local jurisdictions allege that the industry fostered the epidemic by overpromoting its products, while raking in billions as Americans became addicted and overdosed. "To this day," the commission says, "the opioid pharmaceutical industry influences the nation's response to the crisis."

It sure does. In its response to an epidemic that now kills 50,000 Americans a year, the Trump administration wants to spend tens of millions of dollars in part to help the industry responsible sell ostensibly nonaddictive pain medications and "abuse deterrent" opioids that are as addictive as the original opioids.

In a recent speech, President Trump praised a new public-private partnership involving the National Institutes of Health and pharmaceutical companies to develop nonaddictive painkillers and new treatments for addiction and overdoses. "I'll be pushing the concept of nonaddictive painkillers very, very hard," he promised. The N.I.H. says it hasn't set a budget for its "public-private initiative" but spent roughly $600 million on research into pain and opioid use and abuse in 2016.

The federal Centers for Disease Control and Prevention recommends that prescribers avoid opioids for most chronic pain. Experts not affiliated with the pharmaceutical industry urge doctors to make greater use of over-the-counter analgesics and non-pharmacological pain relief methods like physical and spinal manipulative therapies, movement retraining and electrical stimulation.

In September, at a meeting in Trenton with more than a dozen pharmaceutical manufacturers to explore solutions to the crisis, the opioids commission's chairman, Gov. Chris Christie of New Jersey, said developing nonaddictive drugs was a priority. Among the companies he hosted was Purdue Pharma. In late October New Jersey's attorney general joined 10 other states in suing Purdue, owned by the Sackler family, alleging that Purdue deceptively marketed its drug OxyContin as safe for long-term use. "The attorney general makes those judgments, not the governor," Mr. Christie said.

Purdue executives call abuse-deterrent opioids, along with highly effective non-opioid pain products, the "holy grail" for the pharmaceutical industry.

"Abuse-deterrent is a marketing term used to mislead," says Dr. Adriane Fugh-Berman, a pharmacology and physiology professor at Georgetown University who directs PharmedOut, a group that monitors pharmaceutical industry marketing efforts. "At least half of prescribers think that abuse-deterrent means less addictive." It does not; abuse-deterrent pills are simply harder to crush or alter for injection or snorting. "It doesn't prevent you from swallowing them, which is the most common way of abusing opioids," Dr. Fugh-Berman said.

In an email, a Purdue spokesman cited support by the N.I.H., the Food and Drug Administration and the Drug Enforcement Administration for its approach, saying that along with other pharmaceutical companies and "stakeholders" the company believes that "abuse-deterrent technologies can be one of the many effective components of a multipart approach toward combating prescription opioid abuse, misuse and diversion."

Purdue says it supports the C.D.C. guidelines, and its chief executive, Craig Landau, said in Trenton, "I firmly believe there are too many opioids prescribed in this country." True. And Purdue owns a large share of the responsibility for that.

The N.I.H. began its public-private initiative this summer with a series of closed-door meetings with pharmaceutical companies and academics. An N.I.H. spokeswoman, Renate Myles, said the research would include work on non-pharmacological approaches, but "we need to develop new nonaddictive medications for pain. These medications can only be brought to market with the active participation of the pharmaceutical industry."

Purdue participated in the N.I.H. initiative. In June, in response to a call for public comments, J. David Haddox, the company's vice president for policy, sent a letter to the commission outlining Purdue's proposed "policy options," including recommending that the F.D.A. "convert" the opioid market to predominately abuse-deterrent formulations.

The commission's report includes important recommendations like expanding Medicaid coverage for inpatient treatment; expanding treatment with buprenorphine, methadone and other medications, including some still being developed; establishing a national curriculum and standards for opioid prescribers; and expanding an alternative system of drug courts that encourage treatment. Those should be the immediate priorities, not channeling money for more meds to drug companies, from the pockets of Americans whose pain was the industry's gain.

F.D.A. to Expand Medication-Assisted Therapy for Opioid Addicts

BY SHEILA KAPLAN | FEB. 25, 2018

IN AN EFFORT to encourage new treatments for opioid addiction, the Food and Drug Administration plans to begin permitting pharmaceutical companies to sell medications that help temper cravings, even if they don't fully stop addiction.

The change is part of a wider effort to expand access to so-called medication-assisted treatment, or MAT. The agency will issue draft guidelines in the next few weeks. A senior agency official provided details of the proposal to The New York Times.

The new approach was signaled Saturday by the health and human services secretary, Alex M. Azar II, in remarks to the National Governors Association. Mr. Azar said the agency intended "to correct a misconception that patients must achieve total abstinence in order for MAT to be considered effective."

While the Trump administration has generally supported medication-assisted treatment, Mr. Azar's predecessor, Tom Price, was not completely on board with it. Mr. Price caused an uproar among treatment experts when he dismissed some medications that reduce cravings through synthetic opioids last spring as substituting one opioid for another. He subsequently walked back those comments, saying officials should be open to a broad range of treatment options.

Mr. Azar, who took office late last month, said he would work to reduce the stigma associated with addiction and addiction therapy, and would not treat it as a moral failing.

The opioid epidemic is considered the most unrelenting drug crisis in United States history. In 2016, roughly 64,000 people were killed by drug overdoses, including from prescription opioid painkillers and heroin.

Noting federal data showing that only one-third of specialty substance abuse treatment programs offer medication-assisted treatment, Mr. Azar said, "We want to raise that number — in fact, it will be nigh impossible to turn the tide on this epidemic without doing so."

Mr. Azar's comments echo those of the F.D.A. chief, Dr. Scott Gottlieb, who has made battling opioid abuse a priority for his agency. Dr. Gottlieb has moved to reduce opioid prescriptions by doctors and dentists and to promote more medication-assisted treatment, defined as drugs used to stabilize brain chemistry, reduce or block the euphoric effects of opioids, relieve physiological cravings, and normalize body functions.

The F.D.A. has approved three drugs for opioid treatment — buprenorphine (often known by the brand name Suboxone), methadone and naltrexone (known by the brand name Vivitrol) — and says they are safe and effective combined with counseling and other support. But the agency said it would soon publish two guidances, recommendations for drug makers, on the issue.

One encourages the development of new, longer-acting formulations of existing drugs for opioid treatment. The other, which was described in detail to The Times, said new drugs would be eligible for approval that don't end addiction but help with aspects of it, such as cravings, or overdoses, with the goal remaining complete abstinence.

"We will permit an endpoint that shows substantial reductions but does not require the patient to be totally clean at every visit if the measurements are fairly frequent," a senior F.D.A. official said.

The official also said the F.D.A. was seeking medications that can help patients function better and can be helpful when used in combination with therapy and other social support, even if on their own the medications don't completely end addiction. Under the new guidelines, patients and their families will have input in assessing how useful a drug is.

"You could envision different MATs where the different treatments are addressing different aspects of what underlies the addiction, and helping people lead productive lives free from addiction to opioids, even in situations where they still might require replacement therapy," the official said.

Addiction experts were cautious in their praise of the plan, which should be released in March.

"The F.D.A. should keep companies focused on major clinical improvement for patients," said Yngvild Olsen, medical director of the Institutes for Behavior Resources in Baltimore. "A more thoughtful approach to measuring meaningful clinical improvement could expand treatment options, but there is a danger; subjective outcomes that are neither here nor there could encourage the development of products of questionable value."

And Dr. Andrew Kolodny, a director of opioid policy research at Brandeis University, said that the F.D.A. was smart to look for new treatments but that the biggest problem now in treatment wasn't lack of effective medication, but lack of access.

"We already have an effective treatment that people aren't getting access to," he said. "The primary challenge is getting it to people."

As Opioid Prescriptions Fall, Prescriptions for Drugs to Treat Addiction Rise

BY ABBY GOODNOUGH | APRIL 19, 2018

WASHINGTON — The number of new monthly prescriptions for medications that treat opioid addiction nearly doubled over the past two years, according to new data, while prescriptions for opioid painkillers continued to decline.

The changing calculus reflects a stepping up of efforts among policymakers and the medical establishment to address the nation's opioid epidemic, which is killing more than 115 people every day. But it also underscores questions about whether some pain patients are now being undertreated, and whether tightened prescribing over the last few years has contributed to the surge in overdose deaths from heroin and especially fentanyl.

Although the number of people taking medications to combat addiction is rising, it remains a small fraction of the roughly 2.6 million people believed to suffer from "opioid use disorder," or addiction. The federal government has estimated that about 20 percent of them are getting some kind of treatment, but of those, only about a third are getting buprenorphine, naltrexone or methadone, the three medications approved by the Food and Drug Administration.

Prescriptions for opioid painkillers have been dropping since 2011, but the trend accelerated last year with a decline of 10 percent from January through December, according to the IQVIA Institute for Human Data Science, which studies prescription drug use and spending. The highest-dose prescriptions, equivalent to 90 milligrams or more of morphine daily, dropped even more sharply, by 16 percent. Over the course of 2016, high-dose prescriptions dropped by 14.3 percent and opioid prescriptions over all dropped by 1.5 percent.

The number of people newly prescribed opioid pain medicine declined by 7.8 percent over the course of 2017, according to the report, after rising by less than 1 percent the previous year.

The declines come amid a flurry of new insurance company policies and state laws setting limits on opioid prescribing. States have also been tracking opioid prescriptions more closely through electronic databases and requiring more doctors to check the databases for signs of "doctor shopping" or misuse before giving a patient opioids. In New Jersey, the former governor Chris Christie said this year that a new law limiting initial opioid prescriptions there to a five-day supply had led to a 15 percent decrease in overall opioid prescriptions.

Two years ago, the Centers for Disease Control and Prevention released the first national guidelines for prescribing opioids, recommending that doctors try pain relievers like ibuprofen first and that they give most patients only a few days' supply of opioids. Another important development that has helped propel the decline came in 2014, when the federal government tightened prescribing rules for one of the most popular painkillers: hydrocodone combined with a second analgesic, like acetaminophen.

"I think the message is we are seeing measurable impact from all that's going on," said Murray Aitken, executive director of the IQVIA Institute, which published the data as part of a broader report on drug use and spending last year. "These numbers don't tell you what exactly is driving the acceleration in the drop, but we think it's useful to get the 2017 numbers out there so people can see what's happening."

According to the report, prescription opioid volumes peaked in 2011 at the equivalent of 240 billion milligrams of morphine, declining by 29 percent to 171 billion in 2017. Still, that was enough for every American adult to have 52 pills — "a fivefold higher level than in 1992," Mr. Aitken said.

Amid a push by the Trump administration and many states to expand access to medications that help treat addiction by curbing cravings and withdrawal symptoms, the report also found that the number of people newly prescribed these medications, including buprenorphine and naltrexone, nearly doubled over the course of 2017, to 82,000 per month from 42,000.

But Dr. G. Caleb Alexander, co-director of the Johns Hopkins Center for Drug Safety and Effectiveness, cautioned that there was no way of knowing from the data whether the prescriptions came with behavioral therapy and other support, as most experts recommend for people taking addiction medication.

"The issue here is there are startling gaps in quality of care for people receiving medication-assisted treatment," he said. "So it's really important that we do a better job of improving it and building out systems of care that can deliver it en masse."

CHAPTER 5

The Trump Administration vs. Big Pharma

The runaway prices of medicine became a major issue in the 2016 election. Both the Republican and Democratic parties acknowledged that the American people were being harmed by the high prices Big Pharma was charging for prescription drugs. Today, the Trump administration maintains its position on lowering drug prices, but has made little headway in prompting meaningful change. This chapter outlines the Trump administration's positioning to reduce drug prices, protect Medicare beneficiaries and negotiate with the legions of lawyers and lobbyists of Big Pharma.

The Real Reason Medicare Is a Lousy Drug Negotiator: It Can't Say No

BY MARGOT SANGER-KATZ | FEB. 2, 2016

A GOOD NEGOTIATOR needs to be able to walk away.

That is a rule that, surely, Donald Trump knows. And yet in suggesting that Medicare could find big discounts by letting the government negotiate directly over drug prices, he seems to have forgotten it.

Mr. Trump has joined Hillary Clinton and Bernie Sanders in calling for a federal government program to negotiate for Medicare's drug prices. The current system has private insurance companies each negotiating separate deals on behalf of large groups of Medicare patients. Right now, the program is O.K. at negotiating, saving as much as 30 percent off the list price of drugs, according to government reports. But Medicare still pays much, much more than government health systems in other countries.

The idea of government directly negotiating with drug makers has been a liberal favorite ever since Medicare began paying for drugs 10 years ago. You can see the appeal. The thinking goes like this: Medicare's drug plans cover about 37 million people. Maybe if it bargained on behalf of all those beneficiaries as one, instead of dividing them into a series of smaller groups, it could get better deals. Other countries, like Britain, where the government purchases drugs for everyone in bulk, pay much, much less for drugs than the United States. In those countries, private companies don't do the negotiating; the government does. And they don't split the big market.

"We don't do it," Mr. Trump said at a Farmington, N.H., campaign event, according to The Associated Press. "Why? Because of drug companies."

But if you talk to experts who study the pharmaceutical market in the United States, they aren't optimistic that, by itself, letting the government play drug negotiator would take a big bite out of prescription drug spending.

For one, the companies that run the Medicare drug plans aren't really that small, because they also provide drug benefits to companies and individuals with health insurance. The largest pharmacy benefit manager, Express Scripts, covers more than 85 million Americans. Other big pharmacy benefit managers include CVS/Caremark and OptumRx.

But size isn't the only issue. The real problem is that Medicare can very rarely say "No way" to a drug company. Medicare beneficiaries wanted the program to cover most drugs that older people would want to use. So Congress put in place rules that strengthen the hand of the drug companies in negotiations.

Medicare is required to cover almost every cancer treatment that is approved by the Food and Drug Administration, for example, one of six categories where the drug plans can almost never say no to the drug companies. If a drug maker comes out with a new cancer medicine with a sky-high price, there's not much a Medicare plan can do to talk it down.

"If you say, 'We need to get lower prices,' and they just say, 'No,' what are you going to do?" said Walid Gellad, an associate professor of medicine and the co-director of the Center for Pharmaceutical Policy and Prescribing at the University of Pittsburgh.

The Congressional Budget Office has examined several proposals to allow the government to negotiate on drug prices, and it has repeatedly said that the savings would be "negligible" without other major policy changes. Medicare's actuary has reached similar conclusions.

"To negotiate prices any further, the government would need to impose access or coverage restrictions on medicines," said Doug Elmendorf, testifying before Congress in 2009. Elmendorf was the director of the budget office then; he is now the dean of Harvard's John F. Kennedy School of Government.

The government does have one program that can say "no" to drug companies, and it gets much better deals than Medicare. The Department of Veterans Affairs negotiates hard with drug makers. But it is also bound by fewer rules than Medicare, and one result is that it covers far fewer drugs.

A 2011 analysis by Austin Frakt, an economist and Upshot contributor, and two co-authors found that if Medicare limited drugs the way the V.A. does, it could save about $510 in drug spending for every beneficiary every year. But those beneficiaries would lose access to many drugs they were previously taking. In fact, many older patients who get their health insurance from the V.A. also sign up for Medicare drug plans to cover medicines that the V.A. won't.

Other countries act more like the V.A. than Medicare. In Britain, drug makers that won't negotiate won't be able to sell any drugs at all. That's real leverage, but it also means that patients in England don't have access to all the drugs that older people in the United States might want to take.

The trade-offs between price and generosity are real and wrenching. None of the candidates currently talking about allowing Medicare to negotiate for drugs have endorsed allowing Medicare to say no more often. Bernie Sanders's plan strongly suggests that all drugs would be covered with no co-payments at all. Such a plan might make the government a more generous insurer than it is now, but could also result in even higher drug prices.

The Fight Trump Faces Over Drug Prices

BY KATIE THOMAS | JAN. 23, 2017

PRESIDENT TRUMP HAS made it clear that he thinks drug prices are too high and that the pharmaceutical industry, as he put it at a news conference this month, is "getting away with murder."

He joins a host of lawmakers and others who have excoriated drug makers in recent years for high-priced drugs that are out of the reach of many Americans. On Monday, Sean Spicer, Mr. Trump's press secretary, reaffirmed that the issue would be a priority.

One of Mr. Trump's proposals — to force drug makers to bid for the right to sell their products to Medicare beneficiaries — has repeatedly failed to attract enough support in Congress, especially among his fellow Republicans.

"Pharma has a lot of lobbyists and a lot of power, and there is very little bidding," Mr. Trump said at the news conference this month, in comments that briefly sent pharmaceutical stocks tumbling. "We're the largest buyer of drugs in the world, and yet we don't bid properly, and we're going to save billions of dollars."

Polls show that the public is in favor of doing away with a legislative provision that prohibits the federal government from negotiating directly with pharmaceutical companies for drugs that are paid for by Medicare, the government health care program for people who are over 65 or have disabilities.

Removing that prohibition is a favorite cause of liberal politicians like Senator Bernie Sanders of Vermont, but it has been opposed by the pharmaceutical industry and Republicans, including Representative Tom Price of Georgia, the nominee for secretary of health and human services.

Mr. Price declined to say at a confirmation hearing last Wednesday whether he supported Mr. Trump's position, and Democratic senators are likely to question him again on the issue when he appears before the Senate Finance Committee for another hearing on Tuesday.

Whether freeing the government to negotiate on drug prices would lower costs, however, is anything but clear. And its chances of passing a Republican-led Congress are even less so.

WHY CAN'T THE GOVERNMENT HAGGLE WITH DRUG COMPANIES?

Medicare did not cover prescription drugs until 2006, after Congress expanded the program to add a drug benefit, known as Part D. But the measure included something called the noninterference clause, which was backed by the pharmaceutical industry and prevented the federal government from negotiating directly with drug makers.

This prohibition does not mean that pharmaceutical companies can set any price they want. Privately run prescription drug programs, which control the benefits for large groups of Medicare beneficiaries, negotiate on the government's behalf. These programs are run by the same companies — including Express Scripts, CVS and UnitedHealth — that manage the drug plans for large employers and insurers.

WHAT IS THE ARGUMENT FOR REMOVING THIS CLAUSE?

Those who favor letting the federal government negotiate directly on drug prices argue that other countries, including Canada and Britain, already have that leverage with many multinational drug corporations. Their government-run health programs are the only game in town and hold significant power in setting drug prices. Supporters say that if the United States government were allowed to negotiate drug prices for all 41 million Medicare beneficiaries enrolled in drug coverage, it would lead to lower prices across the health care market.

The pharmaceutical industry and Republicans have long opposed such a change, however, saying that significantly cutting payments to drug makers would stifle innovation and prevent them from investing in new lifesaving drugs.

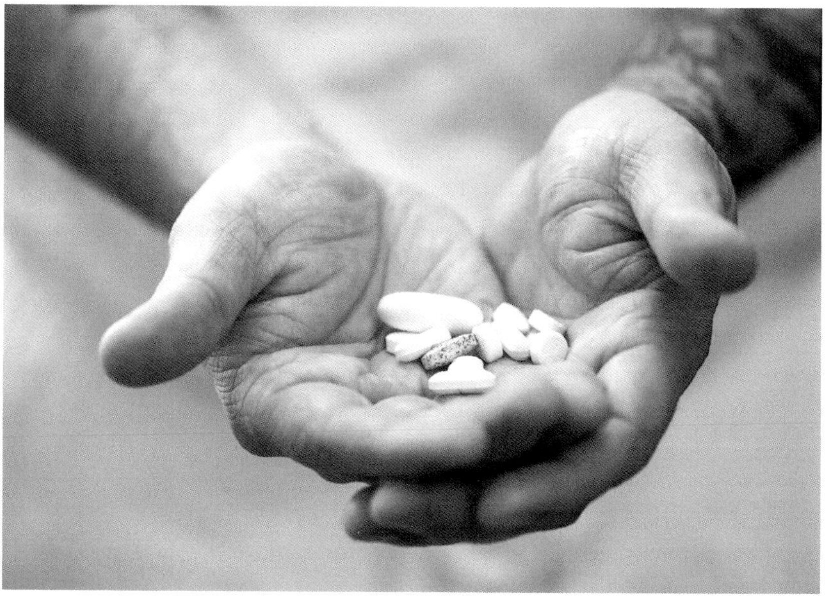

HUNTER MCRAE FOR THE NEW YORK TIMES

President Trump has excoriated pharmaceutical companies for the high price of many drugs.

WOULD NEGOTIATING MEDICARE'S DRUG PRICES ACTUALLY LOWER COSTS?

Many health care experts are skeptical that a repeal of the negotiating ban would have much impact, and certainly not the "billions" of dollars in reductions that Mr. Trump recently promised. The nonpartisan Congressional Budget Office has concluded more than once that a repeal would result in only modest savings, in part because private drug plans are already negotiating on the government's behalf, albeit for smaller pools of beneficiaries.

And even if the ban were repealed, another provision would stand in the way. Under Medicare, the government must cover all drugs in six "protected classes": broad and often expensive treatment areas for patients with conditions such as cancer, depression, epilepsy and H.I.V.

The Veterans Health Administration and the Defense Department are able to negotiate lower prices in part by covering fewer drugs and pitting drug companies against one another.

"You get your largest negotiating power from your ability to walk away," said Dr. Aaron S. Kesselheim, an associate professor at Harvard Medical School who has written frequently on drug prices.

Even if Medicare were to remove those protections and agree to cover fewer drugs — a politically unpopular move that has failed in the past — drug companies might find ways to make up the financial losses, said Dan Mendelson, president of Avalere Health, a consulting firm that works for drug companies, hospitals, insurers and others.

Today's most expensive drugs typically treat rare conditions, like cystic fibrosis and certain types of cancer, for which there are few options. In those cases, drug companies hold the bargaining power, no matter who is on the other side of the table.

"I worry that if you force one price across the market, you may well end up with a higher price in noncompetitive categories than you would otherwise," Mr. Mendelson said.

And even if the negotiating ban were lifted, the United States would still not have the same clout as, say, Britain, whose universal health care coverage makes the government the country's only buyer of drugs.

Some worry that if the United States government were to significantly lower drug prices for Medicare beneficiaries, pharmaceutical companies would respond by raising prices for the millions of people insured through large employers or private insurers. Others contend that if the prices negotiated by Medicare were public, the transparency could level the playing field and lower prices across the board.

WHAT HAS MR. TRUMP'S POSITION BEEN ON DRUG PRICES?

During the campaign, Mr. Trump joined his Democratic opponents, Mr. Sanders and Hillary Clinton, in calling for the federal government to be allowed to negotiate the price of drugs.

After his election, the drug industry exhaled when the health care section of his transition website included more traditional Republican (and industry-friendly) priorities and did not mention the negotiation provision.

In December, Mr. Trump pledged in an interview with Time magazine to bring down drug prices, and this month, he promised to "create new bidding procedures" but did not offer specific details.

WILL SUCH A PROPOSAL EVER CLEAR CONGRESS?

It seems unlikely, given that Republicans control both the House of Representatives and the Senate.

"It's been a nonstarter with Republicans, and it's the traditionally Democratic talking point," said Alana Dovner, a research analyst at Beacon Policy Advisors, which advises investors on developments in Washington. "Something as dramatic as allowing Medicare to negotiate drug prices — that would be such a radical change, and so opposite the traditional Republican health care policies, that it just seems unfathomable at this point."

Mr. Price opposed a Democratic-led measure in 2007, calling it a "solution in search of a problem."

Ms. Dovner and others said that even Democrats were unlikely to support a measure that would allow Medicare to stop covering drugs in protected areas like cancer. A limited effort to do that in 2014 failed amid bipartisan criticism.

"You are by definition saying yes to some drugs and no to others," Mr. Mendelson said. He called that position politically dangerous, saying it would be denounced as "government practice of medicine."

Trump Vows to Ease Rules for Drug Makers, but Again Zeros In on Prices

BY KATIE THOMAS | JAN. 31, 2017

PRESIDENT TRUMP PROMISED some of the nation's top drug company executives in a meeting at the White House on Tuesday that he would slash regulations at the Food and Drug Administration and make it easier for them to manufacture products in the United States.

He also described as "fantastic" the person he planned to nominate for commissioner of the Food and Drug Administration, someone he said would streamline the agency and get drug approval decisions faster.

"You can't get approval for the plant, and you can't get approval for the drug; other than that, you're doing fantastic," Mr. Trump said at the meeting, to laughter from top executives of companies like Merck, Johnson & Johnson, Eli Lilly and Novartis.

But even as he struck a cordial tone with them, he said that lowering drug costs would remain a focus and that he would discuss the issue further during the nonpublic portion of the meeting, away from the news media. "The U.S. drug companies have produced extraordinary results for our country, but the pricing has been astronomical," Mr. Trump said. "We have to get prices down for a lot of reasons."

Battered by public outrage over the rising costs of drugs in recent years, the drug industry has regarded Mr. Trump warily in recent weeks. Pharmaceutical and biotechnology stocks rallied after his election as investors bet that Mr. Trump would reduce corporate taxes and adopt more industry-friendly policies than his Democratic opponent, Hillary Clinton, who had made reducing drug prices a campaign issue.

But that optimism gave way to unease after Mr. Trump pledged to tackle the drug pricing issue himself, including raising the possibility of allowing Medicare to negotiate the prices of drugs directly, something the industry has long opposed.

Just a few weeks ago, Mr. Trump singled out the pharmaceutical industry for its high prices, accusing it of "getting away with murder."

At the meeting Tuesday, Mr. Trump again referred to Medicare's role, saying he would oppose anything that prevented competition, including "price fixing by the biggest dog in the market, Medicare, which is what's happening."

A White House spokesman later clarified that his remarks meant that the president "supports increasing bidding and competition for all drugs in Medicare."

But the president also tried to persuade the executives that he would provide them with assistance, saying: "We can save tens of billions of dollars, and you people are going to do great. You're going to do great."

In comments after the meeting, the drug industry leaders said it had been productive and said they welcomed the president's pledges on cutting regulations and speeding approvals.

But drug safety advocates criticized his comments, saying that eliminating agency regulations would mean rolling back consumer protections on products as diverse as drugs, cosmetics, food and dietary supplements.

"Trump's horrifying proposal reflects utter ignorance about the F.D.A.'s essential role in protecting public health and once again demonstrates his commitment to placing corporate profits above protecting the safety of the American people," said Dr. Michael Carome, director of Public Citizen's health research group.

Dr. Carome said many of the regulations had been set up by Congress so they could not easily be removed. "Most of these regulations, to do away with them would require new statutes and new laws to be passed," he said.

Others said the agency had already loosened the approval process for new drugs in recent years, with questionable benefit.

"Streamlining drug approvals sounds good, but the agency has already weakened approval standards and patients are paying the price — hugely expensive drugs that don't even work," said Diana Zuckerman, president of the National Center for Health Research, a Washington research group that advocates strong safety and efficacy standards. She recently studied expensive new cancer drugs and found that many did not help patients feel better or live longer.

During the meeting, Mr. Trump also told the executives that he was close to naming a candidate to lead the F.D.A.

"You're going to get your products — either approved or not approved — but it's going to be a quick process," he said. "It's not going to take 15 years," apparently a reference not to the length of time it takes the agency to approve drugs but to how long it takes to develop a drug.

He also appeared to express frustration at what he said were unnecessary delays by the agency, especially for drugs that treat patients who are close to death. The agency justifies the delay by saying it needs to evaluate whether the drug is safe, and whether it works, Mr. Trump said: "We can't approve the drug because we don't want to hurt the patient," he said, "but the patient is not going to live more than four weeks."

The Trump administration has not said who the finalists for the position are, but two widely circulated candidates are Dr. Scott Gottlieb, a former F.D.A. official with longstanding ties to the pharmaceutical industry, and Jim O'Neill, an associate of the billionaire Silicon Valley investor Peter Thiel, who has said he favored allowing drugs to be approved even if their efficacy had not been proved.

At the meeting, many of the drug industry leaders were eager to emphasize their long histories in the United States as well as their American manufacturing plants, even though the pharmaceutical industry — like many others — has increasingly moved its production overseas. More than half of the finished drug products that are sold in the United States are made here, according to a recent report in The Wall Street Journal, but the majority of the raw ingredients used to make those products are manufactured in countries like China and India.

Even Joseph Jimenez, the chief executive of the Swiss pharmaceutical giant Novartis, emphasized the company's American ties, pointing out the billions of dollars it spends on research and development and saying, "Our global headquarters is near Boston." Eric Althoff, a spokesman for Novartis, which is based in Basel, Switzerland, said Mr. Jimenez was referring to the company's research and development headquarters.

Mr. Jimenez and others supported Mr. Trump's pledge to cut taxes and regulations. "One of the things that can help us is a lower tax rate," Mr. Jimenez said.

"Yep, we'll get it," Mr. Trump replied.

Drug Lobbyists' Battle Cry Over Prices: Blame the Others

BY ERIC LIPTON AND KATIE THOMAS | MAY 29, 2017

WASHINGTON — Hundreds of independent pharmacists swarmed the House and Senate office buildings one recent afternoon, climbing the marble staircases as they rushed from one appointment to the next, pitching lawmakers on their plan to rein in the soaring drug prices that have enraged American consumers.

As they crowded into lawmakers' offices, describing themselves as the industry's "white hats," they pointed a finger at pharmacy benefit managers like Express Scripts and CVS Health, which handle the drug coverage of millions of Americans.

"Want to reduce prescription drug costs?" the pharmacists argued during their visits. "Pay attention to the middlemen."

A civil war has broken out among the most powerful players in the pharmaceutical industry — including brand-name and generic drug makers, and even your local pharmacists — with each blaming others for the rising price of medicine.

It is an industry that was already spending nearly double what other business sectors in the United States economy allocate on lobbying, and those sums continue to rise. President Trump has only heightened anxiety by accusing the drug industry of "getting away with murder," even though he has not weighed in with his own proposal.

For now, lawmakers are facing an almost daily assault.

"Everyone is very eager to maximize their profits and get a piece of the pie, and sorting it all out is complicated," said Senator Susan Collins, Republican of Maine.

The question is whether a rare confluence of public outrage, political will and presidential leadership can bring about a meaningful change that will slow the drain on consumers' pocketbooks.

"You remember that old photograph of the Three Stooges, their faces cracked sideways and they are pointing at each other?" asked Chester Davis Jr., the president of the Association for Accessible Medicines, sitting in the basement cafeteria of the Russell Senate Office Building at the start of a day in which he would make his own pitches on behalf of generic drug makers. "Everyone is doing the finger-pointing, when in fact there is a lot of blame to go around."

In polls, Democrats and Republicans alike have lowering drug prices near the top of their health care priorities. Public anger has risen along with the skyrocketing prices for many essential medicines — insulin for diabetes, for example, and EpiPens for severe allergic reactions. But will efforts to reduce drug costs surmount the industry's aggressive lobbying and campaign contributions?

"It's still a very uphill fight," said Representative Lloyd Doggett, Democrat of Texas, who like Ms. Collins has been pushing Congress to increase competition and lower prices, "given the millions they have spent on lobbying, advertising and campaign contributions."

With billions in profit on the line, the pharmaceutical and health products industry has already spent $78 million on lobbying in the first quarter of this year, a 14 percent jump over last year, according to the Center for Responsive Politics. The industry pays some 1,100 lobbyists — more than two for each member of Congress.

In the 2016 election cycle, the industry poured more than $58 million into the election campaigns of members of Congress and presidential candidates, as well as other political causes, the Center for Responsive Politics data shows. That was the biggest investment in the industry's history and a 20 percent jump from the last presidential election cycle in 2012.

No single proposal has emerged as a clear winner in the bid to lower prices. Mr. Trump has sent conflicting signals: On one hand, he has accused the industry of "price fixing" and has said the government should be allowed to negotiate the price of drugs covered by Medicare. At other times, he has talked about rolling back regulations and named an industry-friendly former congressman, Tom Price, to head the Department of Health and Human Services, and a former pharmaceutical consultant, Scott Gottlieb, to lead the Food and Drug Administration.

Members of Congress have put forward a grab-bag of options, each of which would help or hurt different industry players.

Some address minor aspects, such as a bipartisan bill that would force brand-name drug makers to hand over samples of their drugs to generic competitors. One would allow for the importing of cheaper drugs. Another would force pharmacy benefit managers to disclose more information about how they did business.

For now, it is a free-for-all.

The brand-name drug industry is the dominant player. It spends the most on campaign contributions, has the largest army of lobbyists and has the biggest pile of chits among lawmakers to try to protect its own interests.

Its trade group, the Pharmaceutical Research and Manufacturers of America, or PhRMA, was so concerned about its vulnerability this year that it increased its annual dues by 50 percent — generating an extra $100 million to flood social media, television stations, as well as newspapers and magazines with advertising that reminds consumers of the industry's role in helping to save lives. A second set of PhRMA ads point blame for price increases elsewhere, like benefit managers and health insurers.

In doing so, PhRMA is seeking to rehabilitate a reputation that was damaged by the actions of companies like Turing Pharmaceuticals, which sharply hiked the price of a decades-old medicine. Its unapologetic former chief executive, Martin Shkreli, came to be seen as the ultimate illustration of the industry's bad deeds.

Though Turing was never a member of the group, PhRMA recently purged nearly two dozen companies from its membership after it voted to exclude investor-driven drug companies like Turing.

Nearly every week that Congress is in session, the industry holds fund-raisers at private clubs and restaurants to help bankroll the re-election campaigns of its allies. One former lobbyist for PhRMA recently boasted that he had once organized six fund-raising events in a two-day period. (He asked that he not be named because the fund-raising efforts are supposed to be confidential.)

In late April, for example, a PhRMA Industry Breakfast was hosted for Representative John Shimkus, Republican of Illinois, at the National Republican Club of Capitol Hill, a members-only hot spot across the street from the Capitol.

The industry had reason to thank Mr. Shimkus. Last year, he helped save pharmaceutical companies billions of dollars by persuading the Obama administration to kill a project that was meant to test ways to lower the cost of the so-called Medicare Part B program, which spent $24.6 billion on prescription drugs in 2015.

Mr. Shimkus, who received nearly $300,000 in drug-industry contributions in the last election cycle, led an effort to collect signatures from 242 members of the House challenging the effort. He also co-sponsored legislation that threatened to block it, which became moot after the Obama administration backed down.

A spokesman for Mr. Shimkus said his actions were intended to protect cancer patients — pointing to a clinic in his district he said might close if the Medicare program had gone into effect — not the pharmaceutical industry.

But other participants said industry influence — as drug companies attempted to preserve their bottom line — had played a decisive role.

"When we first proposed this, people were warning me, 'Be careful, everybody on K Street is going to be gunning for you now,' and I did not really know what they meant," said Andy Slavitt, a top Obama administration official who pushed the prescription drug price experiment. "Now I know. When you take on pharma, you take on this whole town."

Stephen J. Ubl, the chief executive of PhRMA, acknowledged that his group had been "very engaged" in defending his member companies' interests, and blamed a few bad actors — not his own members — for the public's disapproval.

"The researchers wake up every day working for better treatments and cures," he said, echoing his organization's multimillion-dollar advertising campaign, "Go Boldly."

The pharmacy benefit managers are giants themselves. Two of the biggest, Express Scripts and CVS Health, which are among the nation's 50 largest companies, have initiated their own counteroffensive.

In February, Mark Merritt, the president of the Pharmaceutical Care Management Association, the trade group for benefit managers, outlined a strategy to "engage the new administration" and to build "a political firewall on Capitol Hill," according to a confidential memo that was first made public by BuzzFeed.

The memo bragged about the group's courting of senior Trump administration officials. It also said it had met with Capitol Hill staff members and lawmakers, formed a partnership with conservative advocacy groups and created an advertising campaign called "Drug Benefit Solutions."

Last month, the group hosted several hundred government officials and other industry players at a fancy "policy forum" a few blocks from the Capitol, where it detailed just why its members were "uniquely positioned" to save consumers money.

A smaller war is playing out between pharmacy benefit managers and pharmacists, confrontations that have included covert operations.

When the independent pharmacists descended on Capitol Hill in late April, they came with a brochure depicting benefit managers as sharp-toothed dogs, grabbing bags of money.

Yet even as they walked the halls, a group calling itself Ask Your Independent Pharmacist sent a blast email to some of the same lawmakers the pharmacists had just met with. "Whose interests are they on the Hill to champion — the pharmacist's pocketbook or the patients they claim to serve?" an email asked.

When The New York Times called a public relations firm, Kivvit, which operates out of an address listed on the email, staff members repeatedly hung up when asked who had paid for the message. After a reporter called the firm's Chicago headquarters, Tracy Schmaler, a Justice Department aide in the Obama administration who now works at Kivvit, responded: Express Scripts had paid for the message.

Jonah Houts, the head of government affairs at Express Scripts, said the company's role as a middleman drew fire from all sides.

"We were designed to create tension," he said. "We're successful at what we do, and that's why we want to make sure the lawmakers who are considering legislation that affects us understand that."

The generics industry has also come under attack. Though its drugs are generally cheap, some have also risen sharply in price, and prosecutors have been investigating claims of price-fixing by some of the largest players, including Mylan.

Heather Bresch, the chief executive of Mylan and a former chairwoman of the generics trade group, has been pilloried on social media for her role in hiking the price of EpiPens, even though EpiPens sold as branded drugs, not generics.

As the controversy over EpiPens unfolded, Ms. Bresch shifted criticism toward what she called the "broken system" of brokers, distributors and pharmacists who take a cut of the price, too. In January, the generics trade group shed its old name for one that reflects the changed political climate: the Association for Accessible Medicines.

Mr. Doggett, the Texas Democrat, said the industry war was in some ways a positive sign.

"We have moved from 'There is no problem' to 'It's not my fault,' " he said. "It begins to focus attention on what so many of my constituents already know the problem is, which is price gouging."

Draft Order on Drug Prices Proposes Easing Regulations

BY SHEILA KAPLAN AND KATIE THOMAS | JUNE 20, 2017

IN THE EARLY DAYS of his administration, President Trump did not hesitate to bash the drug industry. But a draft of an executive order on drug prices appears to give the pharmaceutical industry much of what it has asked for — and no guarantee that costs to consumers will drop.

The draft, which The New York Times obtained on Tuesday, is light on specifics but clear on philosophy: Easing regulatory hurdles for the drug industry is the best way to get prices down.

The proposals identify some issues that have stoked public outrage — such as the high out-of-pocket costs for medicines — but it largely leaves the drug industry unscathed. In fact, the four-page document contains several proposals that have long been championed by the industry, including strengthening drug makers' monopoly power overseas and scaling back a federal program that requires pharmaceutical companies to give discounts to hospitals and clinics that serve low-income patients.

Mr. Trump has often excoriated the drug industry for high prices, seizing on an issue that stirs the anger of Republicans and Democrats alike. He has accused the industry of "getting away with murder," and said that he wanted to allow the federal government to negotiate directly with drug companies over the price of drugs covered by Medicare.

But the proposed order does little to specifically call out the drug industry and instead focuses on rolling back regulations, a favorite target of the administration across many federal agencies.

"I do believe that the president wants to do something to lower drug prices for people, but this is a far cry from what he said on the campaign trail," said David Mitchell, the founder of Patients for Affordable Drugs, a nonprofit that does not take money from the industry. "I don't see anything there that addresses the drug companies getting away

STEPHEN CROWLEY/THE NEW YORK TIMES

President Trump meeting with leaders from the pharmaceutical industry in January.

with murder, and it appears that is because Pharma has captured the process."

With a new administration in place, the pharmaceutical and health products industry spent $78 million in lobbying in the first quarter, a 14 percent increase over last year, according to the Center for Responsive Politics.

The draft executive order, obtained from an official with knowledge of the proposals, was prepared before last week's meeting of cabinet members and other high-level administration officials. John Czwartacki, a spokesman for the Office of Management and Budget, said the session was the "first of many meetings which will be held throughout the summer," adding that "they will be working to identify both root causes and innovative solutions, leaving no stone unturned."

Many of the people Mr. Trump has hired to work on drug policy have ties to the industry. Joe Grogan, the associate director of health programs in the budget office, worked as the head of federal affairs for Gilead, whose expensive hepatitis C drugs have helped fuel the debate over rising drug costs. Tom Price, the secretary of health and human services, was a Republican congressman whose policies were seen as industry-friendly and who opposed measures like allowing Medicare to negotiate drug prices. And the new commissioner of the Food and Drug Administration, Scott Gottlieb, was a longtime consultant to the drug industry.

Several of the proposals appear to reflect that industry influence. For example, the document directs the United States trade representative to conduct a study of price differences between the United States and other countries, and to review trade agreements that may need to be revised "to promote greater intellectual property protection and competition in the global market."

The pharmaceutical industry has said that Americans pay the highest prices to compensate for low prices in other countries. However, "other countries pay lower prices for drugs in part because their governments control prices," said Allan Coukell, senior director of health programs at the Pew Charitable Trusts. "It's unclear what ability the U.S. would have to change that."

The draft order targets a program, 340B, that requires the drug industry to give discounts to hospitals and clinics that serve large numbers of low-income patients. The industry has complained that the program is being abused, while hospitals say they would have to cut services without it.

"That's one that sticks out as a bit of a head scratcher," said Dr. Joshua M. Sharfstein, a professor at Johns Hopkins Bloomberg School of Public Health who was a top F.D.A. official under President Barack Obama. "This is the executive order to lower drug prices — why would you put in a provision that would raise drug prices?"

In recent weeks, the industry has shown signs it believes it is getting a fairer shake.

In May, Joseph Jimenez, the chief executive of Novartis, told investors that he believed the administration would offer a solution that "will preserve the business model of how we innovate and discover and develop and launch in the U.S., as opposed to some of the bigger and more draconian elements that were discussed earlier," according to Bloomberg.

Dr. Sharfstein and others said they were intrigued by one proposal, known as value-based pricing, that appeals to the industry and policy wonks alike. The idea refers to paying drug companies for the value that a drug brings — refunding money if a drug fails to prevent a costly health condition, for example.

Some proposals appear to address alleviating the rising out-of-pocket costs that patients are being asked to pay. One calls on reducing burdens caused by "regulatory or administrative actions" that cause Medicare beneficiaries to pay the list price for drugs when the companies that run the drug plans — known as pharmacy benefit managers — get a lower price from drug makers. Another would target regulations "that inappropriately or unfairly contribute to higher prices or cost-sharing for medical products for American patients."

Dan Mendelson, president of Avalere Health, a health advisory company whose clients include drug companies and insurers, said, "All of our research shows that when a patient faces high cost-sharing for a drug, they're more likely not to take it."

Still, it was unclear how much issues could be addressed through administrative or regulatory changes. Indeed, many of Mr. Trump's most aggressive statements on the issue — including allowing Medicare to directly negotiate the price of drugs — would require legislative action.

Congress has been consumed by negotiation over the replacement of the Affordable Care Act, and while several drug-pricing bills have been introduced, few have gained much traction so far.

For its part, the F.D.A. is taking action that even Mr. Trump's critics say may well help drive down prices. Mr. Gottlieb is expected this week to announce a new plan to make sure the generic drug approval process isn't being gamed in ways that hamper competition.

Lower Drug Prices: New Proposals Carry Lots of Promises

BY KATIE THOMAS AND REED ABELSON | FEB. 9, 2018

The White House is considering a plan to lower out-of-pocket costs for people in Medicare drug plans, who often pay inflated prices for their drugs.

WHEN IT COMES to high drug prices, President Trump and members of Congress have been long on promises but short on action.

But that appears to be changing: The White House on Friday released a report recommending significant changes that would affect drug costs and the president's budget proposal on Monday is expected to include some plans to expand drug coverage under Medicare. In addition, a spending bill passed by Congress on Friday included a provision that would accelerate closing a payment gap in Medicare for prescription drugs.

The wide-ranging White House report by the Council of Economic Advisers touched on everything from overseas drug pricing to the lack of competition among industry middlemen, laying out a menu of ideas. The report echoed many of the drug industry's complaints; other countries pay unfairly low prices for medicines and cutting profits will stifle breakthroughs.

Mr. Trump's budget proposal is expected to be more specific, including several measures aimed at lowering out-of-pocket spending for people on Medicare (65 and older).

One idea addresses an issue that many consider fundamentally unjust: Consumers are increasingly being asked to pay a greater portion of their drug costs, but they don't get discounts that drug manufacturers offer to health insurers.

The proposal, first floated by federal officials last November, would give at least a portion of that discount to people in Medicare drug plans at the pharmacy counter. The move could lower out-of-pocket costs for people with high drug bills, but would increase the cost of these

Medicare plans, offered by private insurers, for everyone. The idea seems to have the support of the Trump administration, including the new health secretary, Alex M. Azar II, a former Eli Lilly executive.

The proposal, which does not need congressional approval, represents the latest clash between powerful health care industries that are engaged in a war for the moral high ground over rising drug prices. The pharmaceutical industry, backed by influential members of the Trump administration, has been lobbying hard for the change, betting that it would act as an escape valve for patients' anger over drug costs while preserving drug makers' freedom to set any price they want.

By contrast, the insurance companies and pharmacy benefit managers, which oversee drug plans, are loathe to part with what amounts to billions of dollars in rebate windfalls, arguing that it will lead to higher prices.

The change could present a tidy solution for Mr. Trump, who has come under fire for doing little to follow through on his pledge to lower drug prices, even as he has installed several former drug industry executives in prominent government roles. But it would cost the government money — up to $82.1 billion over the next decade, according to its own estimates.

During his address to Congress last month, Mr. Trump reiterated that lowering drug prices was "one of my greatest priorities," and promised: "Prices will come down."

In a press briefing, Mr. Azar signaled his support of passing on rebates to customers. As a government lawyer during the George W. Bush administration, Mr. Azar oversaw the launch of the Medicare drug program.

Insurers' rising use of manufacturer rebates has been a longstanding concern of federal officials, including those in the Obama administration who issued a report on the matter one day before Mr. Trump took office.

Any decision by the federal government is likely to reverberate through the country's health care system, given that many people with employer-provided health insurance are exposed to the same inflated prices. Already, some private insurers are beginning to offer such rebates to customers.

"There's a very basic question here about the role of insurance and health care," said Peter B. Bach, director of the Center for Health Policy and Outcomes at Memorial Sloan Kettering Cancer Center, who supports the change. "We are still uncertain in the United States how much the sick should carry their own weight economically, versus the many should chip in financially to protect those who are sick. That's what this debate is about."

Patients like Antoinette Lopez are the ones caught in the crossfire.

Ms. Lopez, 70, takes Enbrel for rheumatoid arthritis, and she's watched in frustration as her out-of-pocket costs have risen along with the drug's list price. In 2015, she paid $4,547 for 10 months of Enbrel. This year, she expects to pay $5,941 for the same period.

But the insurer that oversees her drug plan, Humana, is pocketing hundreds of dollars every time she fills her prescription from Amgen, which makes Enbrel. Ms. Lopez will never see that money — the rebates are instead applied across the board to keep premiums low for all of the people enrolled in Humana's Medicare plan.

"It's gouging," said Ms. Lopez, a retired nurse administrator from Athens, Ga., who blames insurers and drug makers. "It's despicable."

Humana did not respond to requests for comment, and Amgen said it was "pleased" with the federal proposal.

If Medicare adopts the plan, federal officials estimate that consumers would save, on average, between $45 and $132 a month. But everyone would pay higher premiums, which Medicare estimates would increase anywhere from $14 to $44 a month.

Mark Merritt, chief executive of the Pharmaceutical Care Management Association, the trade group for pharmacy benefit managers, dislikes the proposal and believes the Medicare coverage is a "sound program."

“You don’t want to destabilize the program or inadvertently make things worse,” he said.

But even as Medicare’s drug coverage gets high marks, those who rely on expensive medications are exposed to spiraling drug prices.

Higher prices have led insurers to push more of the cost onto consumers, by imposing high deductibles or requiring that people pay a percentage of a sale price at the pharmacy, not what the insurer pays for the drug after discounts. The administration is expected on Monday to propose placing a cap on out-of-pocket spending in Medicare drug plans, because without one some people pay tens of thousands of dollars a year.

There is a yawning gap between the list price of a drug, which is close to what the consumer typically pays, and the net price, which insurers pay, that is getting larger.

This has led to a huge increase in the amount of the rebates collected by insurers and pharmacy benefit managers.

While insurers contend that most of the rebate money is used to lower premiums, the middlemen also pocket a percentage of those rebates, increasing their profits as the list price rises.

“We’ve built this incredibly complex, hard-to-understand machine,” said Adam J. Fein, president of Pembroke Consulting, a research firm. “Everyone in the system benefits from this pricing strategy, but it’s not necessarily sensible or sending the right price signals to the consumer.”

The pharmaceutical industry says the growing share of rebates is evidence they are working to keep drug costs low. “We are lowering the prices through greater and greater rebates and discounts, and they’re not giving those to patients,” said Robert Zirkelbach, a spokesman for the Pharmaceutical Research and Manufacturers of America, an industry group.

Mark Hamelburg, the senior vice president of federal programs for America’s Health Insurance Plans, the trade group, said the new proposal is little more than a smoke screen by the pharmaceutical industry. “It’s all part of that general effort to change the focus away from the true problem,” he said.

Many who oppose the idea point out that it won’t help everyone because not every drug comes with a large rebate. Many new cancer treatments, as well as products that treat rare diseases, are not discounted at all.

Many of those offering Part D plans say they do not want to raise premiums for everyone to lower the costs for a few. “Mandating rebates be applied at the point of sale would increase costs for the vast majority of seniors in Part D, taxpayers and the government, while benefiting drug manufacturers,” said Carolyn Castel, a spokeswoman for CVS Health, one of the largest pharmacy managers, in an email.

Some large employers have already begun experimenting with offering employees rebates at the pharmacy counter. Despite its opposition to the Medicare proposal, CVS is offering such rebates to commercial clients, like large employers, and has offered the rebates to its employees since 2013.

Ms. Lopez, meanwhile, said she would appreciate some help. Amgen raised the list price of Enbrel by 9.7 percent in January. “I think anything that would make the total costs of high drug costs go down, even if the premiums went up a little bit, would offset it,” she said.

But the solution seems like “some sort of Band-Aid, or temporary, feel-good fix,” she said.

What Big Pharma Fears Most: A Trump Alliance With Democrats to Cut Drug Prices

BY ROBERT PEAR | OCT. 20, 2018

WASHINGTON — The pharmaceutical industry, pilloried by President Trump for the last two years, is war-gaming for the possibility that its worst fear is realized: that Democrats, if they flip control of the House, find common ground with the president to rein in drug prices.

Democrats say they are determined to squeeze the industry's prices and profits, and they have a stack of legislative proposals that could do so. Drug makers are quietly making contingency plans.

"As the midterm elections approach, a feeling of foreboding has settled over the pharmaceutical industry," said John E. McManus, a Republican health care lobbyist whose clients include major drug companies, as well as their trade association, the Pharmaceutical Research and Manufacturers of America.

"Combine the rising blue wave — the Democrat fixation on pharmaceutical pricing — with President Trump's populist focus on getting credit for cutting patients' drug costs, and the industry could be confronting a perfect storm in 2019," Mr. McManus said.

Soon after his election, Mr. Trump bucked his party and accused drug companies of "getting away with murder." In May this year, he unveiled a blueprint to lower drug prices. He followed through this past week with a proposal to force drug companies to disclose list prices in their television advertisements.

Democrats' ideas include allowing Medicare to negotiate lower drug prices; putting a cap on Medicare beneficiaries' out-of-pocket drug costs; requiring manufacturers to disclose and justify any significant price increases; and outlawing tactics used by brand-name drug makers to delay the development and marketing of lower-cost versions of their products.

If Democrats retake the House, the gavel of the Health Subcommittee of the Ways and Means Committee could go to Representative Lloyd Doggett of Texas, an unyielding critic of what he calls price gouging by pharmaceutical companies.

Drug companies say they are counting on the Senate — which political forecasters say is more likely to remain in Republican control — to stop legislation they oppose. But changes are coming there, too.

Pharmaceutical companies will be losing one of their most powerful allies, Senator Orrin G. Hatch, Republican of Utah and the chairman of the Finance Committee, who is retiring after more than 40 years in Congress.

He is likely to be succeeded as chairman by Senator Charles E. Grassley, an Iowa Republican who is more of a populist on health policy. In 2015, he and Senator Ron Wyden, Democrat of Oregon, issued a blistering report on their 18-month investigation of the high prices charged by Gilead Sciences for two hepatitis C drugs.

Mr. Grassley has long supported allowing importation of prescription drugs from Canada — anathema to the industry. He wrote the provisions of federal law that require drug companies to disclose the payments they make to doctors for research, consulting, speaking, travel and entertainment. Mr. Grassley is also the foremost champion of whistle-blower laws, under which drug companies have paid billions of dollars to resolve allegations that they defrauded the government or engaged in illegal marketing practices.

The challenges facing the industry were laid out in stark terms this month by Covington & Burling, a Washington law firm that has been advising pharmaceutical companies for more than 75 years.

Rujul Desai, a lawyer, said in a webinar that the firm had done "war-gaming exercises" with senior drug company executives to prepare them for possible congressional investigations and hearings on drug prices. The goal, he said, is to help clients "communicate the value of their innovative medicines."

One of his colleagues at Covington, Jennifer L. Plitsch, explained how the government could try to use existing laws to force a reduction in the prices of drugs developed with the help of taxpayer funds.

The government has rarely used this authority, Ms. Plitsch said, but that could change. "It is," she said, "a very easy sound bite for price control advocates: Why should American taxpayers both contribute to drug development and then pay the highest prices in the world as patients?"

She suggested how drug companies could answer that argument: "The sound bite is misleading and simplistic. The proposal would chill innovation and hurt patients. A vast majority of the investment in drug development comes from private industry, not the government."

The politics of drug prices cross party lines. Senator Richard J. Durbin of Illinois, the No. 2 Senate Democrat, was among the first to praise Mr. Trump's plan to mandate the inclusion of drug prices in TV ads.

Representative Jan Schakowsky of Illinois, a liberal Democrat, said she was "surprised and happy" to receive a phone call from the Trump administration notifying her of its price-disclosure proposal, which resembles a bill she introduced in July.

"Despite their army of lobbyists," Ms. Schakowsky said, "drug companies should be very, very worried. Drug costs will be one of the first things on our agenda."

Another Democrat poised to pounce is Representative Elijah E. Cummings of Maryland, who is in line to become chairman of the Committee on Oversight and Government Reform if Democrats take control of the House. In the last four years, he has aggressively investigated the industry, peppering drug makers and the Trump administration with numerous requests for information.

Doctors, patients and insurers support many of the efforts to hold down drug costs. Researchers are making significant progress against cancer and other diseases, but "access is meaningless without affordability," said Dr. Victor J. Dzau, the president of the National Academy of Medicine.

Mr. Trump's latest budget would provide Medicare beneficiaries with better protection against high drug costs by limiting their out-of-pocket expenses. Under another Trump proposal that could appeal to Democrats, Medicare beneficiaries would receive more of the savings that insurers extract from drug manufacturers.

The Democrats' proposal for the government to negotiate drug prices for millions of Medicare patients is their preferred solution. But it would also face the most opposition, from drug makers and Republicans who see it as a step toward price controls.

As he campaigned for the presidency, Mr. Trump said he would "negotiate like crazy" to secure lower drug prices for Medicare. The idea — opposed by administration officials who have worked in the pharmaceutical industry — has dropped off his agenda.

"President Trump has seemingly abandoned his campaign promise to have Medicare negotiate like crazy," said Nancy Pelosi, the House Democratic leader. But, she added, "we hope he would work with a Democratic majority to deliver on negotiation authority and lower drug prices."

Drug companies seek to maintain their influence and access in the Capitol with campaign contributions and platoons of lobbyists recruited from both parties.

The drug industry has contributed nearly $12 million to candidates in this year's congressional races, about 60 percent of it to Republicans, according to data compiled by Kaiser Health News. That sum is dwarfed by the $267 million that drug makers report having spent on lobbying in 2017-18, according to the Center for Responsive Politics, an independent group that tracks money in politics.

"Drug companies have been in such a strong position, and they have contributed so generously to people in both parties, they've been pretty well able to block anything," Mr. Doggett said. "But I do believe that there is now a public outcry, a real pent-up demand, that we take action."

Trump Proposes to Lower Drug Prices by Basing Them on Other Countries' Costs

BY ROBERT PEAR | OCT. 25, 2018

WASHINGTON — President Trump proposed on Thursday that Medicare pay for certain prescription drugs based on the prices paid in other advanced industrial countries — a huge change that could save money for the government and for millions of Medicare beneficiaries.

As part of a demonstration project covering half the country, Medicare would establish an "international pricing index" and use it as a benchmark in deciding how much to pay for drugs covered by Part B of Medicare.

"This is a revolutionary change," Mr. Trump said in a speech on Thursday at the Department of Health and Human Services. "Nobody's had the courage to do it, or they just didn't want to do it."

Mr. Trump's announcement was part of a flurry of initiatives emerging from the White House ahead of next month's midterm elections, in which Democrats hope to take control of the House and possibly the Senate. Democrats have focused their campaigns on health care, hammering Republicans on the high cost of prescription drugs and asserting that Republicans would undo protections for people with pre-existing medical conditions — one of the most popular provisions of the Affordable Care Act.

On Thursday, the Trump administration offered an answer — but the drug proposal would take effect in late 2019 or early 2020 at the earliest.

Trump administration officials said they had the authority to use the Center for Medicare and Medicaid Innovation created by the Affordable Care Act to carry out the proposal. That agency has wide discretion to conduct demonstration projects. The Trump administration will

SARAH SILBIGER/THE NEW YORK TIMES

President Trump spoke about prescription drug prices, alongside Alex M. Azar II, the secretary of health and human services, on Thursday.

accept public comments before starting the project. But the proposal will most likely face fierce political resistance from drug makers, some health care providers and some Republicans in Congress, and it could also be subject to legal challenges.

"The administration is imposing foreign price controls from countries with socialized health care systems that deny their citizens access and discourage innovation," said Stephen J. Ubl, the president and chief executive of the Pharmaceutical Research and Manufacturers of America, the main trade group for the industry. He said the proposal would "threaten patient access to innovative lifesaving medicines."

Democrats had their own reasons for skepticism.

"It's hard to take the Trump administration and Republicans seriously about reducing health care costs for seniors two weeks before the election when they have repeatedly advocated for and implemented policies that strip away protections for people with pre-existing conditions and lead to increased health care costs for millions of Americans," said Senator Chuck Schumer of New York, the Democratic leader.

Mr. Trump's announcement came a few hours after his administration released a government study that said Medicare was paying 80 percent more than other advanced industrial countries for some of the most costly physician-administered medicines.

"The current international drug-pricing system has put America in last place," Alex M. Azar II, the secretary of health and human services, said in unveiling the report.

Mr. Trump cited the government's international drug-pricing report in his speech on Thursday, saying he was taking aim at "global free riding" that forces Americans to subsidize drug prices in other countries.

"Americans pay more so that other countries can pay less," Mr. Trump said.

The report compares prices charged by drug manufacturers in the United States and 16 other countries for 27 drugs that are covered by Part B of Medicare.

"Over all," the report said, "prices and reimbursement rates for Part B drugs are significantly higher for U.S. providers than purchasers outside the U.S."

"Medicare could achieve significant savings," it added, "if prices in the U.S. were similar to those of other large market-based economies."

In a Twitter post, Mr. Azar said, "Medicare was found to be paying the highest price for 19 out of the 27 drugs studied." In only one case was Medicare paying less than the international average, he said.

Medicare beneficiaries are generally responsible for 20 percent of the cost of drugs covered by Part B of the program. So if Medicare reduces its payment, the cost to beneficiaries will be "similarly proportionately reduced," the administration said.

However, most beneficiaries now have supplemental insurance, such as a Medigap policy or retiree health benefits, to help pay their share of the bill for drugs covered under Part B of Medicare.

The new method of payment proposed by the Trump administration would be phased in from 2020 to 2025. "Overall savings for American taxpayers and patients are projected to total $17.2 billion over five years," Mr. Azar said.

Among the drugs included in the study were Aranesp, for patients with anemia caused by chemotherapy or chronic kidney disease; several cancer medicines, such as Avastin, Herceptin and Keytruda; Lucentis, for eye conditions that can cause vision loss; and Rituxan, for rheumatoid arthritis and certain types of cancer. The list prices for Keytruda and many other new cancer medicines are substantially more than $100,000 a year. As an example, Mr. Trump said: "One common cancer drug is nearly seven times as expensive for Medicare as it is for other countries. This is a highly used and very effective drug." The president was apparently referring to Treanda, a cancer treatment sold by Teva Pharmaceutical Industries.

The report was notable for several reasons. It uses foreign drug prices as a reference or benchmark to judge prices in the United States. In many foreign countries, officials negotiate prices with drug manufacturers. While Democrats have long pushed for such negotiations, Republicans in this country have blocked them, fearing Medicare could eventually dictate prices or restrict access to drugs deemed to be too expensive.

Mr. Trump campaigned for president on the promise of allowing the government to negotiate drug prices, but then backed away from that position when he unveiled his first drug-price proposals last spring. The new proposal moves back toward that plan, not by having the federal government negotiate drug prices directly, but by piggybacking on price negotiations in other countries.

Foreign countries "use their national health systems to negotiate lower prices in exchange for market access," the Trump administration said in its report.

Democrats were still pushing a more direct route. "On the eve of the midterm elections, the president is proposing a small step on drug price relief when a giant leap is urgently needed," said Representative Peter Welch, Democrat of Vermont. "Instead of nibbling around the edges, he should demand in his State of the Union speech that Congress send to his desk within 30 days a broad price negotiation bill that applies to all drugs in the Medicare program."

Medicare has historically paid 106 percent of the "average sales price" for drugs that patients receive by infusion or injection in doctors' offices. Medicare drug spending has been growing rapidly — at an average rate of about 9.5 percent a year since 2009, according to the Medicare Payment Advisory Commission, an independent agency that advises Congress.

The Trump administration said the current payment formula could provide financial incentives for some doctors and hospitals to use "the highest-priced clinically beneficial product."

The new report acknowledged many "limitations" in the data used for its international price comparisons. The formulation of drugs, their dosage and their strength may differ from country to country, it said.

Prices cited in the study "may not accurately reflect the actual amount paid in the U.S. or abroad," because they generally do not show the effects of rebates offered by drug manufacturers, the report said.

Obama administration officials were also troubled by the rapid growth of spending for drugs covered by Part B of Medicare. In March 2016, they proposed a nationwide experiment to reduce payments for many of these drugs. But they scrapped the plan nine months later after it was criticized by pharmaceutical companies, doctors, patients and members of Congress from both parties, who said it could jeopardize access to important medicines.

Mr. Azar said the Trump administration proposal was "more radical" than Mr. Obama's.

About two-thirds of Part B drug spending is for biotechnology drugs known as biologics.

Countries included in the Trump administration's drug price comparisons, besides the United States, were Austria, Belgium, Canada, the Czech Republic, Finland, France, Germany, Greece, Ireland, Italy, Japan, Portugal, Slovakia, Spain, Sweden and the United Kingdom.

Glossary

active ingredient The molecule or compound in a drug responsible for its therapeutic effect. Other components are considered inactive (or "inert") but do important things, like bind the pill or help extend the release of the medicine into the bloodstream/body.

antidepressant A class of drugs commonly used to treat depressive symptoms and disorders. Some antidepressants are also used to treat anxiety. Examples of antidepressants include Prozac.

Bayh-Dole Act A patent and trademark law amendment that protects exclusivity of new technology and drugs for the entity that owns the patents. The act is supposed to incentivize drug manufacturers to make new therapies because they will be able to make back the money spent on R&D during the time the drug is "exclusive."

blockbuster drug A novel drug that fills a great need in health care and the treatment of disease. These drugs are rare but can earn a drug company millions or billions of dollars.

brand-name drug The original drug developed, marketed and sold by the manufacturer that holds the patent and rights. It enters the market years before generic alternatives are available. This fact is typically reflected in the listed price.

disease branding The effort to prime the market for a new therapy by educating and increasing awareness about a disease.

drug pipeline The planned product line of a drug manufacturer. This includes all the drugs being researched or currently in clinical trials. Not all products in a pipeline will necessarily make it to market.

efficacy The effectiveness of a drug. In clinical trials, a drug needs to show a significant health benefit/improvement over a placebo or drug of similar effect to be deemed efficacious.

EpiPen A medical device that automatically injects an accurate dose of epinephrine (adrenaline) into a patient in case of a life-threatening allergic reaction.

generic drug An identical formulation of a drug manufactured by another company after the patent and exclusive rights of the brand-name drug expires. They are usually set at a lower price than the branded drug.

insurance premium The out-of-pocket cost for a health insurance plan. Insurance companies derive their income from such charges and pay out some of that money to cover the health care claims of their members. These premiums fluctuate based on the rising costs of prescriptions and health care.

National Institutes of Health (N.I.H.) The National Institutes of Health is the federal government agency in charge of public health research. It provides grants and funding to prospective projects in many therapeutic areas, including drug research and development. Within the NIH are many sub-institutes focused on particular disease areas, such as the National Cancer Institute (N.C.I.) or the National Institute of Mental Health (N.I.M.H.).

new molecular entity (N.M.E.) Drugs that contain active ingredients that have not been previously approved. These are considered innovative by FDA standards.

off-label Refers to the use of a drug for a condition other than that for which it was approved by the F.D.A.

opioids Drugs used for pain relief and anesthesia that are also highly addictive.

Pharmaceutical Research and Manufacturers of America The trade group of lawyers and lobbyists that protects the interests of the brand-name pharmaceutical industry in Washington, D.C. Also known as PhRMA.

Media Literacy Terms

"Media literacy" refers to the ability to access, understand, critically assess and create media. The following terms are important components of media literacy, and they will help you critically engage with the articles in this title.

angle The aspect of a news story that a journalist focuses on and develops.

attribution The method by which a source is identified or by which facts and information are assigned to the person who provided them.

balance Principle of journalism that both perspectives of an argument should be presented in a fair way.

bias A disposition of prejudice in favor of a certain idea, person or perspective.

byline Name of the writer, usually placed between the headline and the story.

chronological order Method of writing a story presenting the details of the story in the order in which they occurred.

credibility The quality of being trustworthy and believable, said of a journalistic source.

critical review A type of story that describes an event or work of art, such as a theater performance, film, concert, book, restaurant, radio or television program, exhibition or musical piece, and offers critical assessment of its quality and reception.

editorial Article of opinion or interpretation.

feature story Article designed to entertain as well as to inform.

headline Type, usually 18 point or larger, used to introduce a story.

human interest story Type of story that focuses on individuals and how events or issues affect their life, generally offering a sense of relatability to the reader.

impartiality Principle of journalism that a story should not reflect a journalist's bias and should contain balance.

intention The motive or reason behind something, such as the publication of a news story.

interview story Type of story in which the facts are gathered primarily by interviewing another person or persons.

motive The reason behind something, such as the publication of a news story or a source's perspective on an issue.

news story An article or style of expository writing that reports news, generally in a straightforward fashion and without editorial comment.

op-ed An opinion piece that reflects a prominent individual's opinion on a topic of interest.

paraphrase The summary of an individual's words, with attribution, rather than a direct quotation of their exact words.

quotation The use of an individual's exact words indicated by the use of quotation marks and proper attribution.

reliability The quality of being dependable and accurate, said of a journalistic source.

rhetorical device Technique in writing intending to persuade the reader or communicate a message from a certain perspective.

tone A manner of expression in writing or speech.

Media Literacy Questions

1. Identify the various sources cited in the article "Painkillers Resist Abuse, but Experts Still Worry" (on page 146). How does Alan Schwarz attribute information to each of these sources in his article? How effective are Schwarz's attributions in helping the reader identify his sources?

2. In "Ritalin Wars" (on page 102), Judith Warner uses direct quotes from another article. What are the strengths of the use of a direct quote as opposed to a paraphrase? What are the weaknesses?

3. Compare the headlines of "Drug Goes From $13.50 a Tablet to $750, Overnight" (on page 70) and "Big Price Increase for Tuberculosis Drug Is Rescinded" (on page 75). Which is a more compelling headline, and why? How could the less compelling headline be changed to better draw the reader's interest?

4. What type of story is "Runaway Drug Prices" (on page 61)? Can you identify another article in this collection that is the same type of story? What elements helped you come to your conclusion?

5. Does Margot Sanger-Katz demonstrate the journalistic principle of impartiality in her article "The Real Reason Medicare Is a Lousy Drug Negotiator: It Can't Say No" (on page 174)? If so, how did she do so? If not, what could Sanger-Katz have included to make her article more impartial?

6. The article "Stop Subsidizing Big Pharma" (on page 49) is an example of an op-ed. Identify how Llewellyn Hinkes-Jones's attitude and tone help convey his opinion on the topic.

7. Does "The EpiPen, a Case Study in Health System Dysfunction" (on page 89) use multiple sources? What are the strengths of using multiple sources in a journalistic piece? What are the weaknesses of relying heavily on only one or a few sources?

8. "Grant System Leads Cancer Researchers to Play It Safe" (on page 20) features photographs. What do these photographs add to the article?

9. "Overselling A.D.H.D.: A New Book Exposes Big Pharma's Role" (on page 122) is an example of a critical review. What is the purpose of a critical review? Do you feel this article achieved that purpose?

10. What is the intention of the article "The Insanity of Taxpayer-Funded Addiction" (on page 165)? How effectively does it achieve its intended purpose?

11. Analyze the authors' reporting in "The Fight Trump Faces Over Drug Prices" (on page 178) and "What Big Pharma Fears Most: A Trump Alliance With Democrats to Cut Drug Prices" (on page 202). Do you think one journalist is more balanced in their reporting than the other? If so, why do you think so?

12. Identify each of the sources in "For Profit, Industry Seeks Cancer Drugs" (on page 130) as a primary source or a secondary source. Evaluate the reliability and credibility of each source. How does your evaluation of each source change your perspective on this article?

Citations

All citations in this list are formatted according to the Modern Language Association's (MLA) style guide.

BOOK CITATION

THE NEW YORK TIMES EDITORIAL STAFF. *Big Pharma: The Money Behind the Pills*. New York: New York Times Educational Publishing, 2020.

ONLINE ARTICLE CITATIONS

ALDEN, WILLIAM. "Valeant's History of Deal-Making." *The New York Times*, 21 Apr. 2014, dealbook.nytimes.com/2014/04/21/valeants-history-of-deal-making/.

BERENSON, ALEX. "Blockbuster Drugs Are So Last Century." *The New York Times*, 3 July 2005, www.nytimes.com/2005/07/03/business/yourmoney/blockbuster-drugs-are-so-last-century.html.

BRAY, CHAD. "AstraZeneca to Acquire Majority Stake in Acerta Pharma." *The New York Times*, 21 Dec. 2017, www.nytimes.com/2015/12/18/business/dealbook/astrazeneca-to-acquire-majority-stake-in-acerta-pharma.html.

CARROLL, AARON E. "The EpiPen, a Case Study in Health System Dysfunction." *The New York Times*, 23 Aug. 2016, www.nytimes.com/2016/08/24/upshot/the-epipen-a-case-study-in-health-care-system-dysfunction.html.

CARROLL, AARON E. "$2.6 Billion to Develop a Drug? New Estimate Makes Questionable Assumptions." *The New York Times*, 18 Nov. 2014, www.nytimes.com/2014/11/19/upshot/calculating-the-real-costs-of-developing-a-new-drug.html.

CHEN, PAULINE W., M.D. "Are Doctors Too Wary of Drug Companies?" *The New York Times*, 18 Oct. 2012, well.blogs.nytimes.com/2012/10/18/are-doctors-too-wary-of-drug-companies/.

DELL'ANTONIA, KJ. "Is It Really A.D.H.D. or Just Immaturity?" *The New York Times*, 11 Mar. 2016, well.blogs.nytimes.com/2016/03/11/is-it-really-a-d-h-d-or-just-immaturity/.

GLAZEK, CHRISTOPHER. "The C.E.O. of H.I.V." *The New York Times*, 26 Apr. 2017, www.nytimes.com/2017/04/26/magazine/the-ceo-of-hiv.html.

GOODNOUGH, ABBY. "As Opioid Prescriptions Fall, Prescriptions for Drugs to Treat Addiction" *The New York Times*, 17 Apr. 2018, www.nytimes.com/2018/04/19/health/opioid-prescriptions-addiction.html.

GRADY, DENISE. "F.D.A. Advisory Panel Backs Preventive Use of H.I.V. Drug." *The New York Times*, 10 May 2012, www.nytimes.com/2012/05/11/health/policy/fda-panel-weighs-preventive-use-of-hiv-drug.html.

HINKES-JONES, LLEWELLYN. "Stop Subsidizing Big Pharma." *The New York Times*, 6 Jan. 2015, www.nytimes.com/2015/01/06/opinion/stop-subsidizing-big-pharma.html.

HURLEY, DAN. "Why Are So Few Blockbuster Drugs Invented Today?" *The New York Times*, 13 Nov. 2014, www.nytimes.com/2014/11/16/magazine/why-are-there-so-few-new-drugs-invented-today.html.

KAPLAN, SHEILA. "F.D.A. to Expand Medication-Assisted Therapy for Opioid Addicts." *The New York Times*, 25 Feb. 2018, www.nytimes.com/2018/02/25/science/fda-medication-assisted-therapy.html.

KAPLAN, SHEILA, AND KATIE THOMAS. "Draft Order on Drug Prices Proposes Easing Regulations." *The New York Times*, 20 June 2017, www.nytimes.com/2017/06/20/health/draft-order-on-drug-prices-proposes-easing-regulations.html.

KHULLAR, DHRUV, M.D. "A Profusion of Diagnoses. That's Good and Bad." *The New York Times*, 6 Nov. 2018, www.nytimes.com/2018/11/06/well/live/a-profusion-of-diagnoses-thats-good-and-bad.html.

KOLATA, GINA. "Grant System Leads Cancer Researchers to Play It Safe." *The New York Times*, 27 June 2009, www.nytimes.com/2009/06/28/health/research/28cancer.html.

LIPTON, ERIC, AND KATIE THOMAS. "Drug Lobbyists' Battle Cry Over Prices: Blame the Others." *The New York Times*, 29 May, 2017, www.nytimes.com/2017/05/29/health/drug-lobbyists-battle-cry-over-prices-blame-the-others.html.

MCNEIL, DONALD G., JR. "Advocating Pill, U.S. Signals Shift to Prevent AIDS." *The New York Times*, 14 May 2014, www.nytimes.com/2014/05/15/health/advocating-pill-us-signals-shift-to-prevent-aids.html.

THE NEW YORK TIMES. "Another Drug Pricing Ripoff." *The New York Times*, 20 Jan. 2018, www.nytimes.com/2016/08/25/opinion/another-drug-pricing-ripoff.html.

THE NEW YORK TIMES. "Costly Hepatitis C Drugs for Everyone?" *The New*

York Times, 21 Dec. 2017, www.nytimes.com/2015/09/02/opinion/costly-hepatitis-c-drugs-for-everyone.html.

THE NEW YORK TIMES. "Inflated Drug Prices." *The New York Times*, 21 Dec. 2017, www.nytimes.com/2015/09/14/opinion/inflated-drug-prices.html.

THE NEW YORK TIMES. "The Insanity of Taxpayer-Funded Addiction." *The New York Times*, 11 Nov. 2017, www.nytimes.com/2017/11/10/opinion/opioids-taxpayer-funded-addiction.html.

THE NEW YORK TIMES. "No Justification for High Drug Prices." *The New York Times*, 19 Jan. 2018, www.nytimes.com/2015/12/20/opinion/sunday/no-justification-for-high-drug-prices.html.

THE NEW YORK TIMES. "Runaway Drug Prices." *The New York Times*, 5 May 2015, www.nytimes.com/2015/05/05/opinion/runaway-drug-prices.html.

THE NEW YORK TIMES. "Ways to Fund Research on Rare Diseases." *The New York Times*, 21 Dec. 2017, www.nytimes.com/2015/01/13/opinion/ways-to-fund-research-on-rare-diseases.html.

PEAR, ROBERT. "Trump Proposes to Lower Drug Prices by Basing Them on Other Countries' Costs." *The New York Times*, 25 Oct. 2018, www.nytimes.com/2018/10/25/us/politics/medicare-prescription-drug-costs-trump.html.

PEAR, ROBERT. "What Big Pharma Fears Most: A Trump Alliance With Democrats to Cut Drug Prices." *The New York Times*, 20 Oct. 2018, www.nytimes.com/2018/10/20/us/politics/trump-pharmaceutical-industry-healthcare.html.

POLLACK, ANDREW. "Big Price Increase for Tuberculosis Drug Is Rescinded." *The New York Times*, 21 Dec. 2017, www.nytimes.com/2015/09/22/business/big-price-increase-for-tb-drug-is-rescinded.html.

POLLACK, ANDREW. "Drug Goes From $13.50 a Tablet to $750, Overnight." *The New York Times*, 20 Sept. 2015, www.nytimes.com/2015/09/21/business/a-huge-overnight-increase-in-a-drugs-price-raises-protests.html.

POLLACK, ANDREW. "For Profit, Industry Seeks Cancer Drugs." *The New York Times*, 2 Sept. 2009, www.nytimes.com/2009/09/02/health/research/02cancerdrug.html.

POLLACK, ANDREW. "New Cholesterol Drugs Are Vastly Overpriced, Analysis Says." *The New York Times*, 21 Dec. 2017, www.nytimes.com/2015/09/09/business/new-cholesterol-drugs-are-vastly-overpriced-analysis-says.html.

POLLACK, ANDREW. "Senators Condemn Big Price Increases for Drugs." *The New York Times*, 21 Dec. 2017, www.nytimes.com/2015/12/10/business/senators-condemn-big-price-increases-for-drugs.html.

POLLACK, ANDREW. "Valeant Under Investigation for Its Drug Pricing

Practices." *The New York Times*, 19 Jan. 2018, www.nytimes.com/2015/10/15/business/valeant-under-investigation-for-its-drug-pricing-practices.html.

POLLACK, ANDREW, AND MICHAEL J. DE LA MERCED. "Roche to Buy InterMune for $8.3 Billion." *The New York Times*, 24 Aug. 2014, https://dealbook.nytimes.com/2014/08/24/roche-to-buy-drug-maker-intermune-for-8-3-billion/.

RAE-DUPREE, JANET. "When Academia Puts Profit Ahead of Wonder." *The New York Times*, 6 Sept. 2008, www.nytimes.com/2008/09/07/technology/07unbox.html.

ROSENTHAL, ELISABETH. "The Lesson of EpiPens: Why Drug Prices Spike, Again and Again." *The New York Times*, 2 Sept. 2016, www.nytimes.com/2016/09/04/opinion/sunday/the-lesson-of-epipens-why-drug-prices-spike-again-and-again.html.

SANGER-KATZ, MARGOT. "The Real Reason Medicare Is a Lousy Drug Negotiator: It Can't Say No." *The New York Times*, 2 Feb. 2016, www.nytimes.com/2016/02/02/upshot/the-real-reason-medicare-is-a-lousy-drug-negotiator-it-cant-say-no.html.

SCHOTT, BEN. "Disease Branding." *The New York Times*, 18 Oct. 2010, schott.blogs.nytimes.com/2010/10/18/disease-branding/.

SCHWARZ, ALAN. "Painkillers Resist Abuse, but Experts Still Worry." *The New York Times*, 21 Dec. 2017, www.nytimes.com/2015/06/07/us/painkillers-resist-abuse-but-experts-still-worry.html.

SCHWARZ, ALAN, AND SARAH COHEN. "A.D.H.D. Seen in 11% of U.S. Children as Diagnoses Rise." *The New York Times*, 1 Apr. 2013, www.nytimes.com/2013/04/01/health/more-diagnoses-of-hyperactivity-causing-concern.html.

SILBERMAN, STEVE. "Overselling A.D.H.D.: A New Book Exposes Big Pharma's Role." *The New York Times*, 20 Jan. 2018, www.nytimes.com/2016/08/28/books/review/adhd-nation-alan-schwarz.html.

SMITH, DANIEL. "It's Still the 'Age of Anxiety.' Or Is It?" *The New York Times*, 14 Jan. 2012, opinionator.blogs.nytimes.com/2012/01/14/its-still-the-age-of-anxiety-or-is-it/.

SOLOMON, STEVEN DAVIDOFF. "Explaining Valeant: The Main Theories." *The New York Times*, 19 Jan. 2018, www.nytimes.com/2016/03/30/business/dealbook/explaining-valeant-the-main-theories.html.

THOMAS, KATIE. "The Complex Math Behind Spiraling Prescription Drug Prices." *The New York Times*, 21 Dec. 2017, www.nytimes.com/2016/08/25/business/high-drug-prices-explained-epipen-heart-medications.html.

THOMAS, KATIE. "The Fight Trump Faces Over Drug Prices." *The New York Times*, 23 Jan. 2017, www.nytimes.com/2017/01/23/health/the-fight-trump-faces-over-drug-prices.html.

THOMAS, KATIE. "Ruling in Off-Label Marketing Case Is a Win for Drug Makers." *The New York Times*, 3 Dec. 2012, www.nytimes.com/2012/12/04/business/ruling-backs-drug-industry-on-off-label-marketing.html.

THOMAS, KATIE. "Trump Vows to Ease Rules for Drug Makers, but Again Zeros In on Prices." *The New York Times*, 31 Jan. 2017, www.nytimes.com/2017/01/31/health/trump-vows-to-ease-rules-for-drug-makers-but-prices-remain-a-focus.html.

THOMAS, KATIE, AND REED ABELSON. "Lower Drug Prices: New Proposals Carry Lots of Promises." *The New York Times*, 9 Feb. 2018, www.nytimes.com/2018/02/09/health/trump-drug-prices-medicare.html.

WARNER, JUDITH. "Ritalin Wars." *The New York Times*, 15 Nov. 2007, opinionator.blogs.nytimes.com/2007/11/15/ritalin-wars/.

Index

This book is current up until the time of printing. For the most up-to-date reporting, visit www.nytimes.com.